Acting Edition

Slave Play

by Jeremy O. Harris

∥SAMUEL FRENCH∥

Copyright © 2023 by Jeremy O. Harris
All Rights Reserved

SLAVE PLAY is fully protected under the copyright laws of the United States of America, the British Commonwealth, including Canada, and all member countries of the Berne Convention for the Protection of Literary and Artistic Works, the Universal Copyright Convention, and/or the World Trade Organization conforming to the Agreement on Trade Related Aspects of Intellectual Property Rights. All rights, including professional and amateur stage productions, recitation, lecturing, public reading, motion picture, radio broadcasting, television, online/digital production, and the rights of translation into foreign languages are strictly reserved.

ISBN 978-0-573-70878-7

www.concordtheatricals.com
www.concordtheatricals.co.uk

FOR PRODUCTION INQUIRIES

UNITED STATES AND CANADA
info@concordtheatricals.com
1-866-979-0447

UNITED KINGDOM AND EUROPE
licensing@concordtheatricals.co.uk
020-7054-7298

Each title is subject to availability from Concord Theatricals Corp., depending upon country of performance. Please be aware that *SLAVE PLAY* may not be licensed by Concord Theatricals Corp. in your territory. Professional and amateur producers should contact the nearest Concord Theatricals Corp. office or licensing partner to verify availability.

CAUTION: Professional and amateur producers are hereby warned that *SLAVE PLAY* is subject to a licensing fee. The purchase, renting, lending or use of this book does not constitute a license to perform this title(s), which license must be obtained from Concord Theatricals Corp. prior to any performance. Performance of this title(s) without a license is a violation of federal law and may subject the producer and/or presenter of such performances to civil penalties. Both amateurs and professionals considering a production are strongly advised to apply to the appropriate agent before starting rehearsals, advertising, or booking a theatre. A licensing fee must be paid whether the title(s) is presented for charity or gain and whether or not admission is charged. Professional/Stock licensing fees are quoted upon application to Concord Theatricals Corp.

This work is published by Samuel French, an imprint of Concord Theatricals Corp.

No one shall make any changes in this title(s) for the purpose of production. No part of this book may be reproduced, stored in a retrieval system, scanned, uploaded, or transmitted in any form, by any means, now known or yet to be invented, including mechanical, electronic, digital, photocopying, recording, videotaping, or otherwise, without the prior written permission of the publisher. No one shall share this title(s), or any part of this title(s), through any social media or file hosting websites.

For all inquiries regarding motion picture, television, online/digital and other media rights, please contact Concord Theatricals Corp.

MUSIC AND THIRD-PARTY MATERIALS USE NOTE

Licensees are solely responsible for obtaining formal written permission from copyright owners to use copyrighted music and/or other copyrighted third-party materials (e.g., artworks, logos) in the performance of this play and are strongly cautioned to do so. If no such permission is obtained by the licensee, then the licensee must use only original music and materials that the licensee owns and controls. Licensees are solely responsible and liable for clearances of all third-party copyrighted materials, including without limitation music, and shall indemnify the copyright owners of the play(s) and their licensing agent, Concord Theatricals Corp., against any costs, expenses, losses and liabilities arising from the use of such copyrighted third-party materials by licensees. For music, please contact the appropriate music licensing authority in your territory for the rights to any incidental music.

IMPORTANT BILLING AND CREDIT REQUIREMENTS

If you have obtained performance rights to this title, please refer to your licensing agreement for important billing and credit requirements.

SLAVE PLAY received its world premiere at New York Theatre Workshop (James C. Nicola, Artistic Director; Jeremy Blocker, Managing Director) in New York, New York, on November 19, 2018. The production was directed by Robert O'Hara, with scenic design by Clint Ramos, costume design by Dede Ayite, lighting design by Jiyoun Chang, sound design and original music by Lindsay Jones, movement direction by Byron Easley, intimacy direction and fight direction by Claire Warden, and dramaturgy by Amauta Marston-Firmino. The stage manager was Jhanaë K-C Bonnick. The cast was as follows:

KANEISHA	Teyonah Parris
JIM	Paul Alexander Nolan
PHILLIP	Sullivan Jones
ALANA	Annie McNamara
DUSTIN	James Cusati-Moyer
GARY	Ato Blankson-Wood
TEÁ	Chalia La Tour
PATRICIA	Irene Sofa Lucio

This production of *SLAVE PLAY* opened on Broadway on October 9, 2019, at the Golden Theatre, a Shubert Organization Theatre (Philip J. Smith, Chairman; Robert E. Wankel, President). It was produced by Seaview Productions; Troy Carter; Level Forward; Nine Stories; Sing Out, Louise! Productions; Shooting Star Productions; Roth-Manella Productions; Carlin Katler Productions; Cohen Hopkins Productions; Thomas Laub; Blair Russell; WEB Productions; Salman Al-Rashid; Jeremy O. Harris; Mark Shacket, Executive Producer; and New York Theatre Workshop. The creative team and cast remained the same as the NYTW production, except for the following cast change:

KANEISHA	Joaquina Kalukango

CHARACTERS

KANEISHA – (28) A dark, black woman unafraid of what she knows she wants.

JIM – (35) A white man and inheritor of more than he knows how to handle.

PHILLIP – (30) A mulatto who still has to learn his color.

ALANA – (36) A white woman who wants more than the world sees fit to give her.

DUSTIN – (28) A white man but the lowest type of white – dingy, an off-white.

GARY – (27) A dark, black man whose life has been lived with the full trauma of his color.

TEÁ – (26) a mulatto who is studied in her black and her white.

PATRICIA – (30) A light brown woman who knows many lives.

SETTING

MacGregor Plantation, a few miles south of Richmond, Virginia

NOTES ON STYLE

SLAVE PLAY is a comedy of sorts. It should be played as such. I'm not sure where the music is coming from but it's there. You should not work to make the audience comfortable with what they are witnessing at all.

The events of the play are happening in real time. There shouldn't be so much scene "transitions," the action of the play should just fall into the next moment. A (//) in the text delineates a dynamic shift in present location to a new location on the plantation.

Southern accents should be used, deeply and broadly, until they are not. You will know when.

Perhaps the spaces on the MacGregor Plantation are literalized with deep verisimilitude (this is preferred in some ways) but if they are not they should be presented with the bareness of a black box. An aesthetic that will telegraph to an audience: "If only they had more money, but they are doing what they can..."

This is a play about shades, colors as much as it's about race. Color play, shade play, should be of interest to those casting this piece. What does it mean if Gary isn't "blue-black" (in the words of Toni Morrison) but just "black black"? Does it change his relationship to the space? In my mind yes, but I haven't seen this "black black" Gary's audition yet.

Everything in life is a performance. I've chosen to present a performance of antebellum life that is in conversation with the ways in which that time has been presented to and informed the world's collective imagination of life in the American South during slavery.

*For Maxwell Neely-Cohen,
on the occassion of his thirtieth birthday,
the only person who will love this play.*

ACT I

"Work"

(The lights slowly rise on the cramped quarters of the MacGregor Plantation's overseer's cottage.)

(A metal framed bed with a feather mattress sits in a room to the side of a large open space that houses a nineteenth-century bachelor's kitchen and a table full of fruits and vegetables in a basket with two chairs before a large black bear-skinned rug.)

*(We watch as **KANEISHA**, a slave, casually [and badly] sweeps the floor of the open living area. Looking down and over distrustfully at the bear-skin rug between broom strokes.)*

(Suddenly, from above, Rihanna's "Work" begins to play.)

*(**KANEISHA** looks up, as though in recognition, a smile appearing then disappearing from her face – she goes back to sweeping.)*

(Yet soon the sounds of this faraway island girl get beneath her skin, in her spine, her legs, her bottom and she is dancing. More specifically, she is twerking and suddenly the broom is out of her hand and on the floor.)

(Her ass moves up and down in revelry as she hikes up her coarse cotton dress and bends into a dutty wine.)

(Her hands move up to the scarf that wraps her impressive natural afro and she frees her hair of its clutches.)

(Suddenly Drake is singing and she's on the ground... she throws her hands before her and begins to pop – her staccato undulation in perfect time with Drake's delivery.)

*(Behind her a door opens and standing in the light of the bright Virginia sun is **JIM**, the overseer, in overalls and a straw hat holding a large thick whip. He stares at her for a moment before clearing his throat.)*

*(The music abruptly shuts off and **KANEISHA** is still there pop pop pop popping.)*

JIM. KANEISHA!
The hell you doin?

*(With an inhalation **KANEISHA** is up and staring back at **JIM** – prey before predator. She puts the scarf back on her head, hiding away her hair.)*

KANEISHA. Oh lord...
...
Uh...
...
...
I's sorry Massa Jim.
...
...
Somethin jus came ova me.

JIM. It's somethin alright!
  I ain't never seen no
  "negress"
  move like that there before!

   (**JIM** *shifts to hide his growing tumescence.*)

  Where'd you learn dat?
  Thought they beat all the Africa outcha'll
  fore we broughtcha up here to MacGregor's.

KANEISHA. Well Massa / Ji–

JIM. *(Confused whisper.)* Ain't gotta call me
  "Massa"
  I don't reckon.

   (An awkward pause.)

KANEISHA. ...
  ...
  I –
  I thank
  I do...
  Massa Jim.

JIM. Really?
  ...
  ...
  Naw, see I'm the overseer
  I oversee.
  ...
  ...
  I don't own ya.
  That's
  ya know
  that's
  Master MacGregor.

JIM. Up in the big house.
MASTER.
MacGregor.
I's just...

KANEISHA. OK Massa –
I mean "Jim"...
I just...
Ain't there some sorta...?
I guess...
...
...
...
um...
Mista?
Mista Jim?
Is that better?

JIM. Mista Jim's alright.

KANEISHA. OK...
Mista Jim.
...
...
Um...
yeah...
What I was tryin to say
was that
yes...
y'all did,
when they brought us ova –
y'all did
try to tear it way from us.
The truth of our bodies?
The way they moved
Our bodies.

Told us it
was
devilish
Our bodies
told us that it won't
fit
for civ'lized eyes
Our bodies,
movin like dat
But…
But…
I guess…
I don't know?
Some of it still.
It's just in me?
In my blood?
My legs?
My body?

>(**JIM** *was trying to listen, but he still can't get over the exchange they just had.*)

JIM. Yeah…
 …
 …
 …
Kaneisha,
I just,
um,
I wantcha to know that the only reason I didn't wantcha callin me "Massa"
was cause
you know,
cause it bothers
me.

KANEISHA. Um...
   aight
   Mista
   Jim.

JIM. It's just kind of annoyin?
   Don't seem quite fair,
   You see?
   To put me in the same category
   as them folk.
   Big House Folk.
   We in this little shed,
   basically.
   I ain't
   fancy!
   Like the MacGregors
   up in their
   big ol house.
   ...
   ...

   (He laughs.)

Naw
Me?
All I own is this little plot of God's green that we on right now
And I had to work that off...
Might as well be a nigga m'self.
Only difference is
I
you know?
I's sorta your manager.

KANEISHA. OK...

JIM. So...
    yeah.
    It's different!
    "Massa."
    Just.
    This
    yeah /
    I don't (know about any of –)

KANEISHA. Well I'm sorry Mista Jim.
    I'm truly truly / sorry and I –

JIM. There ain't no reason to / be sorry Kaneisha

KANEISHA. Don't know what to do about that offense.
    ...
    ...
    ...
    It's just something,
    when I sees a white man...
    They...
    I don't know...
    ...
    ...
    I mean,
    you is
    bout to beat me now
    ain'tcha?
    And that's –
    I don't know...?
    ...
    Something
    usually
    makes a man feel like "MASTER"
    is the title / he deserves...

JIM. What makes you think I'm bout to beatcha?

KANEISHA. Well you got that whip, ain'tcha?

> *(An awkwardly long pause.)*

JIM. Oh.
yeah...
this...

> *(He looks at his whip.)*

...
...
Well I am bout to beatcha.
...
...
that's true.
Told ya hours ago,
"I get back? I want my property
all of it,
PRISTINE,
real pretty-like,
want it so clean you can eat off the ground
without gettin
lint
or
crumbs
or
nothing like that on your tongue.
...
...
Not even dirt!
Don't want to see it!
Didn't want to see it!
Want to be able to take off my shoes and walk round

barefoot
and not look down at my feet
and see the soles of them to be black.
NO!
Don't want black feet.
Don't want em at all.
Not even outside.
Yet,
Uh,
Here I am,
back in my house
and the outside:
spotless,
pristine,
pretty-like.
The porch, even:
spotless,
pristine,
pretty-like.
I walk up,
look around,
I've got a big ol smile on my face,
thinking,
"Well I know she new
but maybe Kaneisha ain't gonna be
another
uh
another,

> *(He begins to use the whip to shake loose a thought that's stuck.)*

…

…

JIM. another useless,
uh
hefer!
Yes!
Another useless hefer
like the rest of em.
But then I come in…
I open my door
and I see you,
down on your knees
dancing like
like uh
a damn,
raccoon in heat.

> (**KANEISHA** *lets out a small laugh but recovers quickly.*)
>
> *(He moves toward her.)*

And I'm thinking to myself,
the hell?
Then I look down at my floor and there's dirt everywhere
and I know…
You know,
I have this whip.
This,
you know
maybe this the only way she gone learn
and I thought you had promise!
You were bout to surprise me!
But look at this
this whole room is disgusting.
Now if you were me,
what might you do?

Given the circumstance...
what might you do?

    (**KANEISHA** *looks around awkwardly.*)

KANEISHA. ...
    ...
    ...
    ...

JIM. Kaneisha?

KANEISHA. Oh!
    You,
    you actually wan
    an answer?

JIM. I asked a question ain't I?

KANEISHA. Oh!
    Well...
    I mean...
    If I was you
    I don't think –
    I don't think
    I'd wanna beat myself, Mista Jim.
    That,
    to me,
    that ain't something I'd wanna do.
    But I ain'tchu sir.
    I...
    yeah...
    ...
    ...
    I don't know what I'm sposed to say.

JIM. You think this here flo is clean girl!

KANEISHA. It ain't dirty sir.

JIM. But is it clean?

KANEISHA. I –

JIM. Would you eat off this here floor?

KANEISHA. Like a dog?

JIM. Yes,
like a dog.
Would you eat off this floor like a dog?

KANEISHA. ...
...
I –
I reckon I would.
It ain't dirty by my estimation sir.

> (**JIM** *looks at her, he walks over to the table and grabs a cantaloupe from the table. He throws it upon the ground, it explodes.*)

JIM. You'd eat that watermelon there off the ground?

> (**KANEISHA** *looks down at the cantaloupe and back up at* **JIM**, *then back at the cantaloupe.*)

KANEISHA. The cantaloupe?

JIM. The watermelon.

KANEISHA. That's a cantaloupe, Mista.

JIM. No it ain't,
it's a watermelon.

> (*He looks down at it.*)
>
> (*Long pause.*)

Ain't it?
Coulda sworn that was a...

KANEISHA. Watermelons are green,
on the outside,
they green.
Red in the middle.
...
...
...

JIM. What the hell's a cantaloupe?

KANEISHA. What you just threw on the ground?

JIM. The hell...

KANEISHA. Cantaloupes are
white on the outside
and orange / on the inside.

JIM. Oh.
Well the cantaloupe.
You eat that cantaloupe off the ground?

>   (**KANEISHA** *looks down at it.*)

KANEISHA. I mean...
I said I would.

JIM. Well gone head then.
Get down there an eat if the floor's so clean.
Then maybe I'll spare ya from a beating this time.

>   (**KANEISHA** *keeps looking.*)

>   (**JIM** *cracks the whip.*)

Gone now!

KANEISHA. I don't really like the taste of cantaloupe...

>   (*An awkward pause.*)

JIM. What?

KANEISHA. The taste?
Cantaloupe sorta
it's sort of empty in your mouth.
It ain't sweet the way it should be
it sort of taste like the color of its skin.
White.
It don't much taste like orange.
The way you imagine orange spose to taste
it just sits there
like this block of nothing.

(Awkward pause.)

JIM. And?

KANEISHA. ...

*(**JIM** cracks the whip again.)*

*(**KANEISHA** looks up at him and inhales.)*

(She gets on her knees and bends down and begins to eat the cantaloupe.)

JIM. You like that?

*(**KANEISHA** continues to eat.)*

Is it still sitting in your mouth
all empty
and disgusting?
All "white"?

*(**KANEISHA** eats.)*

You don't like the way white tastes too much huh?

*(**KANEISHA** begins to eat more ferociously. As though she likes it.)*

> (*Slowly, subtly, moans begin to escape her mouth and her bum begins to wiggle like a dog wagging her tail.*)

Oh…
or maybe you do.
You sho'll is clearing it all up down there.
Like you like it.
Like you think the floor is real clean.
Clean as a plate.
Pretty.
Pristine.
Is that what you think?

> (**KANEISHA** *moans in the affirmative, looking up at him. She's eaten all the big chunks by now. Her bum is still moving in a sort of twerk en retard.*)

> (**JIM** *is barely hiding his stares or his tumescence.*)

I see you're
you're
you're
you're jigabooing again.

> (**KANEISHA** *looks up at him.*)

Doing whatever it is you were doing before.
It's –
Do it like you were doing it when I came in.

KANEISHA. What do you mean Mista Jim?

JIM. I mean…
make your behind bounce
up like it was before.
Jigabooing this way and that.

KANEISHA. Like this?

(**KANEISHA** *does it.*)

JIM. Exactly like that.

KANEISHA. I can't really control it Mista Jim.
Is this bad?
You gone beat me for this Mista Jim?
For moving like this?

JIM. No I ain't gone beatcha.

KANEISHA. You ain't?

JIM. Nah...
you
you've cleaned up the way you was supposed to.
You done ate off the floor,
you done proved to me that you ain't like them others.

KANEISHA. You don't think I'm a lazy negress Massa –
I mean, MISTA Jim?

JIM. I think you beautiful Kaneisha.
Look at what you doing to me

(*He takes her hand and places it on his erection.*)

KANEISHA. Oh Mista Jim!

(*He pulls her up to her feet and begins to kiss her deeply. He starts to pull up her dress and pull down his pants.*)

JIM. Kaneisha!

KANEISHA. Mista Jim,
call me a nasty negress.
A nasty, lazy negress.

(**JIM** *turns her around and guides her toward the bear-skin rug. He pulls up the back of her dress and gets right next to her ear.*)

JIM. I know you can't read,
bout how bout I just spell it with my tongue?

(He puts his head between her legs.)

(**KANEISHA** *lets out a sigh of disappointment.*)

//

(Bright Virginia light crashes into the boudoir of Madame MacGregor. **ALANA**, *a woman in her thirties, but far from done... stands fanning herself and unbuttoning, then rebuttoning her bodice.)*

(She moves from her vanity to her four-poster bed, onto which she flops. Yet after a moment she still can't get comfortable there. Still too hot. She walks over to the window and throws it open. Letting her head out to breathe in the afternoon light and breeze.)

(Finally somewhat comfortable, she walks over to her daybed and sits again, more regally, and cleans up her hair.)

ALANA. *(Yelling offstage.)* Phillip!
Phillip, your mistress needs you.
I got an itch only you can scratch!

(From far off we can hear someone making their way up the stairs of a grand house.)

(Suddenly, **PHILLIP**, *a young mulatto man with an imposing countenance, enters the boudoir in a smart tux with tails.)*

PHILLIP. Mistress?
You called?

ALANA. *(Still fanning herself.)* Phillip!
This heat wave is sending me down a well of unease
and I'm at a loss for what to do.
...
I tried to ready myself for a day in town by getting dressed
putting on my makeup, jewels,
but now town feels so far
and I, too tired.
...
Then, I thought I'd busy myself with a game!
One of the ones me and mammy used to play with each other
when I was a girl?
But "Clean the Pickaninny" ain't much fun by your lonesome.
...
Then I thought I'd read a book,
but every book is the same:
"A man is sad"
"A man is sad so he builds a cabin"
"A man is sad so he finds a wife"
"A man is sad so he leaves his wife"
"A man is sad so he befriends an injun"
"A man is sad so he kills an injun"
"A man is sad"
"A man is sad"
"A man is sad"

(She flops back on her daybed.)

PHILLIP. I'm sorry to hear bout that Mistress.

ALANA. Then I remembered,
"I always feel so calm when Phillip is playing me songs on his little fiddle."
So I thought to get you to play something for me.
Would you like that?

(**PHILLIP** *smiles, uneasy.*)

PHILLIP. I thought I won't llowed to play when Massa MacGregor won't home.
Massa MacGregor say he don't want me makin no mulatto magic.
Say mulattos was gifted with music to woo whites away from they God-given paths.

ALANA. Oh nonsense!
That man is so superstitious!
Anyway,
mulattos ain't the ones with magic.
Any magic a mulatto has was spent on their flesh.
Obviously.
That Africa voodoo is all over them real black uns,
The ones straight from Africa.
That's why mama always said if they're blacker than the night
and can't count to ten
without gruntin like a gorilla
then you don't let em on your land.
The gorilla niggas are the ones who cast the spells.
Everybody knows that.

(**ALANA** *fans herself more furiously.*)

PHILLIP. ...

ALANA. So go on in there and get that fiddle.
Let me hear something.
Settle my mind a bit.

PHILLIP. Yessuh Mistress.

> (**PHILLIP** *exits.*)

> (**ALANA** *stands up and looks around her boudoir.*)

ALANA. "Mulatto magic"!
Who's ever heard of such a thing...
Half-breeds have no witchcraft.
...
...
Or do they?
...
...

> (*She looks out the door, concerned.*)

No...

> (*She is attacked by another flash of hot and begins to unbotton her bodice once again.*)

> (**PHILLIP** *re-enters with a violin.*)

PHILLIP. Mistress? Where would you like me to / stand –

ALANA. (*Pointing to the window.*) Turn around!
My bodice is undone!

> (**PHILLIP** *does.*)

Go right there!
Next to the window,
So your notes can ride on the breeze
and cool my breast
and my mind.
But don't turn around!
I don't want to you to see...
It's just...
it's so hot.

PHILLIP. Yessuh Mistress.

> (**PHILLIP** *walks with his back to* **ALANA** *all the way to the window, the Virginia sun beating down on his brow.*)
>
> (*He begins to tune the violin.*)

ALANA. Oh Phillip!
No!

PHILLIP. Oh I's sorry Mistress.
I was just trying to make sure it sounded nice.
Gettin it in tune for you.

ALANA. Please don't.
That ghastly sound moves up my spine and stays there.
It's quite unpleasant.

PHILLIP. Yes Mistress.

> (**PHILLIP** *inhales and begins to play a beautiful rendition of Beethoven's Op. 132.*)
>
> (*He's very good.*)
>
> (*The music does seem to dance upon the breeze as he plays and his body moves with an unencumbered freedom that exists in those who were born to play.*)

ALANA. Stop!

> (**PHILLIP** *stops abruptly and looks back at her, before catching himself and looking forward.*)

PHILLIP. Yes Mistress?

ALANA. Why are you playing that European garbage?
That Mozart
or whatever
you know that's Master / MacGregor's favorite not –

PHILLIP. It's Beethoven, Mistress.

ALANA. Beethoven,
Mozart,
Chopin,
They are all the same.
Long boring notes.
NO!
That's –
...
...
...
What I wanna hear is some of the negro music you play for the ladies down at y'all's cabin.
I can hear y'all some nights
when I'm laying in bed
hooting and hollering
having a good ol time.
Nobody has a good time listening to BEETHOVEN.
They suffer through it.
Cause it's new!
But NO.
I want something that will actually ease my mind.
Play me some of your music.
A negro spiritual!

PHILLIP. A negro spiritual?

ALANA. Or whatever it is that you play for all of them down there...
I hear how the negresses bray and swoon from up here...
I'd love to see you
Playing something like...
something like that for once
up here.

Instead of this stuffy European nonsense.
Don't that sound nice?
Being able to play something honest for once?
Something you actually like?

> (**PHILLIP** *shifts uncomfortably.*)

PHILLIP. But I like Beethoven.

ALANA. ...

...
Well I don't.
So play something that'll make me hoot and holla like the negresses outside waiting to rut on ya later.

PHILLIP. Yes, Mistress.
I –
I think I can do that.

> (**PHILLIP** *lifts his violin again. This time he looks forward and begins to expertly play a song that sounds somewhat familiar, but alien at the same time.*)
>
> (*The tune moves through the wind and up and around* **ALANA**'s *chest. The smoothing familiarity encouraging the beginning of a dance.*)

ALANA. Oh Phillip,
this,
this is beautiful.
This is so beautiful.
What's it called?

PHILLIP. Um...
I don't know.
It's just come to me.

(Yet, by now, the tune's familiarity should finally be syncing up with the musical ear of any person born after the 1970s in America.)

*(As **PHILLIP** tosses himself into full revelry while playing the chorus we start to hear in the notes the chorus to "Pony" by Ginuwine.)*

*(**ALANA** is moving around the room, the song has finally taken her over. She undoes her hair and unbuttons her bodice more. She is dancing wildly, her dress slowly falling off her as she moves this way and that, revealing dark black lingerie underneath.)*

ALANA. I love this!

I've never heard nothing like this in my life!

(Suddenly, she's dancing in just her lingerie and the heels she had on beneath her dress, like an antebellum Jamie Lee Curtis dancing in True Lies.*)*

*(She throws herself onto **PHILLIP**, who is still not looking behind him, her head against his back, grinding on him. She grinds like this until **PHILLIP** sets down the violin.)*

Oh Phillip!

My husband was right.

You

you done...

You done cast some sort of mulatto spell on me!

Spun my head up in a circle so that all I can think of is you

every facet of you.

(He turns around, concerned.)

PHILLIP. Oh no, Mistress!

I don't know how that's possible!

> (*Seeing her naked body, he covers his eyes.*)

My apologies, Mistress.
I knew Massa didn't have no reason to lie to us!
Oh lord!

> (**ALANA** *takes his hands into hers and looks into his eyes.*)

ALANA. I like this spell tho.

PHILLIP. Naw hush that up Mistress!
You done let my devilish mulatto music weave its way into
your impish female brain,
and lord knows it's bigger than mine own
but it's still weak
in the ways a woman's mind often is.

> (**ALANA** *starts to laugh.*)

What's so funny Mistress?

ALANA. Whatever this spell is doesn't make me feel like a woman tho.

PHILLIP. What do you mean?

ALANA. You've wrapped me up in some spell that's left me garish!

> (**ALANA** *sniffs* **PHILLIP**.)

Set that fiddle down.

> (**PHILLIP** *does.*)

I want to be inside you.

PHILLIP. What, Mistress?

ALANA. I want to be inside you!
  Ain't that queer?
  This spell you done weaved with
  this mulatto music you conjured up
  has done my head in.

PHILLIP. I don't know what you mean Mistress but / you –

> (**ALANA** *kisses him. Deeply and passionately. He's larger than her, but she's very much in control of all of this.*)

ALANA. Lie down on the bed.

PHILLIP. Mistress?
  Ain't Massa gettin / home soon?

ALANA. I don't care.
  Lie.
  Down.

PHILLIP. Yes Mistress.

> (**PHILLIP** *lies down on the bed.*)

> (**ALANA** *walks to her vanity and pulls out a long ebony dildo. She smiles.*)

ALANA. On the night before my wedding,
  my mother gave me this
  told me, "That MacGregor boy is nice
  he'll take good care of you,
  but he'll never please you
  the MacGregor men, they ain't pleasers…
  That's why so many of their women end up lying with mandingos.
  That's why they have all them stables of mulattos
  and quadroons and octoroons
  and so many trees full of noose'd up bucks

cause the men,
bless their hearts,
The men don't have much to give the women.
So take this.
It's been my only deterrent from the mandingos,
and it was my mother's before me.
Take it and use it when you need it."

>   (**ALANA** *smiles.*)

But!
I've never felt a need to use it.
Not really.
Never really felt like it much fit with me.
And I'm perfectly satisfied being unsatisfied.
Or at least I thought I was…

>   (**PHILLIP** *looks at* **ALANA** *as she caresses the large ebony dildo, rubbing some oil from her bedside table on it.*)

PHILLIP. Do you want me to –?
On you Mistress?

ALANA. Oh no Phillip!
I saw clear as day what I wanted you to do with this as you played that song
and started casting that spell…
…
…
Take off your pants.

PHILLIP. Mistress?

ALANA. Take em off.
That's it.
Like that.

(**PHILLIP** *lies on the bed pantsless.* **ALANA** *takes a moment to admire him.*)

PHILLIP. Now what Mistress?

ALANA. Now turn over.

(**ALANA** *sits on the bed as* **PHILLIP** *turns over and begins to slowly kiss and lick his bottom.*)

Being the man is so much fun.

(**PHILLIP** *moans.*)

Do you like being the woman Phillip?

PHILLIP. I'm not sure, Mistress.

ALANA. Do you like this?

(*Slowly,* **ALANA** *begins to push the dildo into* **PHILLIP**. **PHILLIP** *moans with pleasure and pain.*)

PHILLIP. Ahhhhh

ALANA. You like this?

PHILLIP. I'm not sure, Mistress.

//

(*The mid-afternoon Virginia sun snakes its way through stacked-up bales of hay in the MacGregor plantation's barn. The residue from a recent horse feeding is strewn across the ground.*)

(*A white indentured servant,* **DUSTIN**, *enters with a heavy bale of hay and stops short just before a new pile that is being stacked. Winded, he sits down and fans himself for a second.*)

> *(Just as he sets his head in his hands, **NIGGER GARY**, a slave wearing a straw hat and fine boots beneath a manicured pair of cotton pants and shirt, enters.)*

GARY. Boy!
Ain't resting time yet.

DUSTIN. Oh,
I was just tired so I sat down for a second.
I'll get back to it lickity split.

GARY. Lickity split was before boy.
Getcha ass up now, I said!

DUSTIN. Yes sir.

> *(**GARY** begins to laugh.)*

What is it?

GARY. "Yessir"?
HA!
"Yessir"!
…
…
…

> *(**DUSTIN** gets up and begins adding his bale to the stack.)*

You's a funny white man.
"Yessir"
Is that what they teach y'all
"indentured servants"?

DUSTIN. You're in charge ain'tcha?
I say "yessir" to the mens in charge.
White, black whatever.
You's the man in charge.

GARY. I guess I am.
That's what Massa MacGregor told me.
I's in charge.
But
that's what makes you a funny white man.
Ha!
Ain't used to seein them allow
no nigga to run they show.
You's a funny white man.
They look atchu and they must barely see ya as white.
And I don't either to be quite honest.
So...
now I'm at a bit of
A
what's the word?
A quandary?
A query?
Summin with a "qu" sound.
But now
I
Don't know what I should call ya.

DUSTIN. My name is Dustin.

GARY. I know ya name is "Dustin."
Dustin!
Dustin!
That's bout the only white thing aboutcha,
Dustin!
But what should I call ya?

DUSTIN. Your name is Gary.
That's pretty white too don'tcha think?

GARY. It's Nigger Gary.
My name is Nigger Gary.

DUSTIN. Alright, "Nigger Gary"...
>but the only "nigger" thang about your name
>is the title before Gary.
>Otherwise you'd just sound like any ol white overseer.
>"You see Gary movin about them hefers yesterday?
>Gary with blond hair,
>blue eyes,
>steely countenance.
>You see whicha way Gary took them bucks and hefers?
>Gotta love good ol White Gary.
>Good ol boy
>just like the rest of us.
>Gary of the Blond Hair
>Gary of Blue Eyes
>
>>*(He begins to laugh.)*
>
>Gary of the Pinkened Scrotum!"

GARY. That's enough of that,
>Duh!
>Stin!
>
>>*(He kicks down the bale of hay **DUSTIN** just sat atop the others.)*
>
>>*(**DUSTIN** and **NIGGER GARY** both look at it then at each other.)*

DUSTIN. ...
>...
>...
>...
>...
>...
>...
>OK...?

GARY. ...
>...
>...
>...
>...
>...
>...
>Why you just standing there
>Dustin?
>Get it on up!

DUSTIN. ...
>...
>...

GARY. I said get it up!

>*(**GARY** kicks him down.)*

DUSTIN. Ow!

GARY. Watcha ow'ing about
>Dustin?!
>That should feel normal for ya.
>Shouldn't it?
>Seeing how you ain't nothing but a white man
>waiting for a good dusting
>of MY BOOT!

DUSTIN. What?

GARY. That's what you are!
>That's what I'm goin to call ya...
>"Boot Dustin"!

DUSTIN. Boot Dustin?
>That doesn't make any sense!
>That / is –

GARY. IT DOES!
If I say it does
it do!
Your body only fit for a nigga's boot dustin
so you Boot Dustin!
...
...
Pick up that hay Boot Dustin.

>   (**DUSTIN** *just looks up at him.*)

DUSTIN. ...
...
...
...

GARY. What's your problem Boot Dustin?
You done gone retard Boot Dustin?
You stricken with paralysis Boot Dustin?
Is this what indentured servitude look like Boot Dustin?
Is that what that term means?
I can't read so I can't look it up in a book
but what I seem to be understanding is that INDENTURED SERVANT IS DEFINED AS AN INEFFECTUAL, UNINTELLIGIBLE WHITE!
DOES THAT SOUND BOUT RIGHT BOOT DUSTIN?
YOU COM / PREHEND –

>   (*"Multi-Love" by Unknown Mortal Orchestra begins to play, stopping* **GARY** *mid-speech.* **GARY** *looks up angry and annoyed before scoffing.*)

>   (*Suddenly, with a scream,* **DUSTIN** *is up and tackling* **GARY** *[ideally when the percussion hits].*)

*(They are wrestling and fighting for control. One moment **DUSTIN** is atop **GARY**, throwing blows down on his chest and face. The next is **GARY** on top sending blows down to **DUSTIN**.)*

(As the melee'd pas de deux kicks up more dust and hay from the barn floor, suddenly the movements become more and more erotic. Shirts begins to fly off. Hands begin reaching for belts. Pants fly off revealing matching Calvin Kleins or like...2(X)IST?)

(Bloodied faces begin colliding, open mouths swallowing chins and noses and ears and missing mouths completely.)

*(This goes on for quite a while until **DUSTIN** breaks away and looks at **GARY**, who is just wearing his boots, underwear, and hat.)*

(The song ends.)

DUSTIN. What the hell you think you doin Nigger Gary?
You're disgusting.
Could have you lynched for deigning to touch me like that.
You can talk to me anyway you please.
But when it comes to touch?
I ain't "Boot Dustin."
I'm Dustin The White
who can have your nigga slave ass hung up
and tied out for touching me like that
daring to,
hoping to...

GARY. Is that so?

DUSTIN. That's so.

GARY. What about if you touch?

> (**DUSTIN** *walks over to* **NIGGER GARY** *and licks his face.*)

DUSTIN. I can touch wherever I please.
With whatever I please.

GARY. You right.
And I can say whatever I want!
However I want!

DUSTIN. Guess those be the powers our races have bestowed us.

> (**DUSTIN** *puts his hand in* **GARY***'s underwear, squeezing his balls tightly but gently.*)

GARY. Boot Dustin?

DUSTIN. You sure you wanna call me that while I'm here, holding you in my hands?

GARY. I's still your manager.
Massa MacGregor would be quite upset if his favorite buck
was sterilized by some erstwhile
...
...
um...
...
Indentured servant!

> (**DUSTIN** *begins to laugh.*)
>
> (*He can't stop laughing.*)
>
> (*He laughs and laughs and laughs until* **GARY** *is infected with the laughter too.*)

DUSTIN. What?
"esterwhile...
...

DUSTIN. um...
   ..."
what were you trying to say?

GARY. I don't know.

> (**GARY** and **DUSTIN** collect themselves and stare at each other.)
>
> (Breathing each other in.)
>
> (**DUSTIN** reaches over and kisses **GARY**.)

Boot Dustin?
This is nice.
Real nice.
But I'd like it better if you did it the way you was meanta.

DUSTIN. What do you mean?

GARY. I mean
I want you to do whatchu were just doing.
Throwing your tongue
up
down
around my mouth?
I want you to do that
...
...
...
but on your knees.
Get on your knees
and open your mouth
close your eyes
and let your tongue
dance around what it finds there.

> (**DUSTIN** smiles.)

DUSTIN. Alright.

Whatever you say Nigger Gary.

> (**DUSTIN** *gets on his knees. A Virginia breeze sending strands of hay through the barn in a burst.*)
>
> (*He opens his mouth, his face next to* **GARY**'s *crotch.*)
>
> (**GARY** *inhales and takes a step back. His hands on his waist.*)
>
> (**DUSTIN** *closes his eyes and moves his tongue out of his mouth. Flicking it this way and that.*)
>
> (**GARY** *lifts up his well-booted foot and places it on* **DUSTIN**'s *mouth and* **DUSTIN** *begins to clean his boot with his tongue.*)
>
> (**GARY** *shivers and shakes, writhing ever so slightly as* **DUSTIN** *gets more and more into it, his hands by his side, his face and tongue doing all the work as* **GARY** *stands in what can best be described as "The Captain Morgan."*)

(*Licking.*) Uhhh...
uhhh...
so yummy
...
this big
black thing.
...
...
you taste of leather.
...
...

DUSTIN. of dirt.

...

...

Of the earth...

...

...

uhhhhh

...

...

...

I always imagined the taste of dirt
on one of you

...

...

...

but never the taste of grass
of soot
of all the elements of God's green.

>   (**GARY** *is shivering intensely now.*)
>
>   (*It is about to happen. He is fully erect in his little undies at this moment.*)

GARY. Uh huh

...

...

uh huh.
uh huh.
fuck.
fuck.
fuck.
oh god.
Oh god.
OHHHHH GODDDDDDD!!!

(He comes.)

*(**GARY** falls down and begins to weep.)*

*(**DUSTIN** opens his eyes.)*

DUSTIN. Oh fuck!
Gary?
Gary.
Fuck.
Uhhh...
Can someone help?
HELP!

//

*(**PHILLIP** and **ALANA** sit on opposite sides of the bed not looking at each other.)*

(They are both semi-dressed.)

ALANA. My husband will be home soon.
You should clean up here
fore he gets home!
Get one of those negresses from the yard.

PHILLIP. Alana...

ALANA. Mistress!

PHILLIP. Mistress.

...
...
...

Massa ain't coming back.

ALANA. This isn't time for your mulatto tomfoolery Phillip.

PHILLIP. You don't have a husband Alana.

ALANA. Mistress!

PHILLIP. Mistress.

>*(The Virginia breeze moves through the boudoir, blowing papers through the room.)*

>*(**PHILLIP** stands up and goes to his violin.)*

ALANA. It's finally cool'd down in here Phillip!
Ain't that nice?
To be free of the heat for a moment.

>*(**PHILLIP** begins to play the Beethoven again as he walks out into the hall.)*

Phillip!
No more please?
You know how European music rattles my nerves!

>*(**PHILLIP** continues to play as he moves through the house.)*

>//

>*(**KANEISHA** is on all fours, **JIM** behind her thrusting wildly. She is nearing a space of ecstasy.)*

KANEISHA. That's...
yes
yes
yes
yes
YES!

JIM. YOU LIKE THAT?

KANEISHA. I love this.

JIM. You do?
Kaneisha you do?

KANEISHA. Call me negress.

JIM. Kaneisha.
Oh Kaneisha you feel so good.
So right...

KANEISHA. Negress!
Mista Jim
please
Negress!

JIM. You feel so good
so good
so
good
...
...
uh...
...
Ne
...
...
...
Negress!
You feel so
so
good Negress.

(As he says this his thrusts become more and more contained.)

KANEISHA. Yes!
Yes, fuck yes!
That's exactly what I –
what I –
Mista Jim
Massa
Massa Jim

KANEISHA. I
 I
 I
 fuck
 fuck
 are you gonna whip me if I come Massa Jim?
 Are you gonna whip me?
 For being a nasty negress?
 For being your disgusting little bed wench?
 Huh?
 Huh?

 (She is nearing her climax.)

JIM. I
 I
 I

 *(**JIM** has almost completely stopped thrusting at this point.)*

KANEISHA. Are you gonna beat me like the dirty
 little –
 wait
 wait
 Mista Jim.
 Why?
 Why you gone all / soft all of

JIM. *(In a full British accent)* Kaneisha…
 Kaneisha I'm sorry.
 But.
 …
 …
 I
 …

...
This doesn't work for me

KANEISHA. No

no

no

no / no

NO!

JIM. starbucks?

starbucks...

Starbucks.

Starbucks!

STARBUCKS!

STARBUCKS!

STARBUCKS!

> (**JIM** *stands up and begins putting back on his clothes as* **KANEISHA** *looks up at him, dejected.*)

> (*Suddenly, the doors burst open, and two young women,* **PATRICIA** *and* **TEÁ**, *rush in.*)

PATRICIA. Oh my god.

You two were making such good progress!

TEÁ. I know,

like,

I was so excited for you two.

> (**KANEISHA** *bursts into tears.*)

> (**JIM** *just puts on his clothes silently, not looking at either.*)

No,

no

that wasn't meant to trigger.

TEÁ. I apologize.
   You all did wonderful work.

PATRICIA. Yes.
   Truly
   so brave.

TEÁ. I think we all should take a little breather?

PATRICIA. Yes.

TEÁ. Let's meet back in the big house in fifteen?
   How's that sound you two?

   (**KANEISHA** *nods.*)

   Jim?
   Jim?
   How does that sound?

   (**JIM** *stands up and walks out of the room.*)

End of Act I

ACT II

"Process"

(Lights up on the main house of the MacGregor Plantation. It is outfitted with all the fittings of modernity but still feels haunted by the antebellum south.)

(JIM, KANEISHA, ALANA, PHILLIP, GARY, and **DUSTIN** *sit in a semi-circle in modern-day leisurewear eating snacks and drinking water, nervously looking around at each other.)*

(Note: Another option is that over the intermission each of the couples enters the space at different paces in various states of undress.)

(It should be noted as well that **JIM** *is British,* **KANEISHA** *speaks in a natural Southern dialect, but none of the others are from the South and henceforth speak in their natural accents.)*

(TEÁ and **PATRICIA** *enter and sit down on either side of them on the floor. They both have iPads in their laps. From time to time they look down at their iPad as though reading a note.)*

(ALANA *does the same but with a notebook she has that is filled to the brim with notes and bookmarks.)*

TEÁ. OK partners,
so
um…
let's like…
process?
OK?
Um…
…
…
Day Four!
…
…
Wow…
Day.
Four.
I think it's really important to reiterate
that
what we all just explored
was incredibly difficult
and triggering,
but it was also fantasy.
Right?
And like,
fantasy is complex
and it is multifaceted
and it is real.
Like real
REAL.
It's our earliest form of processing.
You know?
Like,
there is a true…
what's the word?

PATRICIA. Materiality?

TEÁ. Yes!
Thank you Patricia.

PATRICIA. You're welcome T.

TEÁ. There's a real materiality
to our psychic spaces.
And Day Four is all about
manipulating those psychic spaces
like the raw material they are
in order to process
the ANHEDONIA, right?
The emotional numbing
that's brought us all here
together,
In this room.
But
again,
just like…
Um…
Just like anything
that's raw
it's going to leave us tender!
And that's therapy right?
Therapy is all about pushing ourselves
outside of our comfort zone so that we can tenderize
the scars that have started to form.

PATRICIA. Exactly!
And since our Day Four
Fantasy Play was cut
short / we all

PHILLIP. Who cut it short?

*(A chorus erupts of: "Exactly!" "That's what I wanna know," from everyone but **KANEISHA** and **JIM**.)*

ALANA. / Did someone say "Starbucks"?

TEÁ. I don't think that matters.

PATRICIA. Over the next hour things are going to be hard.
There's a lot of processing that needs to happen.
And processing / is a –

JIM. Can you stop saying processing?
We aren't computers.
My emotions aren't materials.

PATRICIA. Great note Jim.
Really great note.
I'm going to proces–
I apologize.
Ruminate on that.
But you are heard.
You are affirmed
and I see you.

*(**JIM** sighs and shifts uncomfortably. He looks at **KANEISHA**, who is staring intently at **TEÁ** and **PATRICIA**.)*

TEÁ. So let's begin unpacking, OK?
While it's still hot for all of us…
How does that feel?
Who wants to go first?

*(**PATRICIA** and **TEÁ** each open a new window on their iPads in preparation to take notes on what is being said.)*

(The group is silent.)

...
...
...
...
...

> (**TEÁ** *reaches below her seat and grabs a box of tissues and walks over to the middle of the circle and places them there.*)
>
> (*She walks back to her seat.*)

...
...
...
...
...
...
...
...

PATRICIA. There's no right or wrong way to enter into this, everyone.

...
...
...
...

OK...
um,
would it help if
Teá or I facillitated / some questions?

TEÁ. And if that –

> (*Recognizing her mistake.*)

Oh my god I'm so sorry I made that intervention Patricia.

PATRICIA. It's fine.

TEÁ. No it's not, for me, Patricia.
Know that I was hearing you.

PATRICIA. I know.

TEÁ. OK...

>   (*Back to the group.*)

I was going to say that...
I um
I like
recognize the fact
that even offering to
um,
"facilitate"?
could feel reductive to you all
at this raw moment
so if you still need a few / more min–

DUSTIN. Gary came.

...
...
...

TEÁ. Alright!
OK.
Yes.
Gary came.
I wasn't sure from just listening, but,
yes,
Gary came.
And
that's amazing.
Let's –

>   (**TEÁ** *and* **PATRICIA** *begin a silent "deaf clap."*)

PATRICIA. *(Scribbling on her digital notebook.)* And how did that feel for you Dustin?

(**DUSTIN** *looks to* **GARY**, *who is looking down.*)

DUSTIN. Ummmm
well
it
was
it's
yeah...
um,
it was complicated.

GARY. ...
...
...

PATRICIA. Complicated is good.

DUSTIN. I guess?

PATRICIA. What specifically felt complicated to you?

DUSTIN. I...
ummm...
I –

GARY. He didn't like having to be "white."

DUSTIN. Fuck you Gary.

GARY. It's true.

DUSTIN. You were crying.
That's what worried me.
That's the –
you know, fuck you.
You were crying / as you came.

TEÁ. Let's not engage with "fuck yous" right now partners.

TEÁ. Let's keep this open for now.
There will be time for aggression later.

DUSTIN. He got really into it.
It didn't feel like "fantasy" a lot of the time
it felt like personal?
Or / like...

GARY. What?

DUSTIN. You got too into it!

GARY. It takes two to tango baby.

DUSTIN. ...
...

GARY. But, yeah.
I came.
And...
yeah.
I um.
I liked it?
I felt it?
I...
enjoyed it.

    (**GARY** *begins to cry.*)

TEÁ. OK.
OK.
So we're there.

    (**ALANA** *reaches over and rubs* **GARY***'s back with a smile.*)

PATRICIA. Yes,
exactly.
We're all in that raw, nasty place.
But that's OK.

Anhedonia,
as you all know
makes it impossible for us to be in any sort of place with another person...
raw, nasty, or otherwise.
So this is a breakthrough.
One worth being proud of because you were able to get to that place,
/ together.

ALANA. *(Standing up.)* Honestly, it was just hot to me.
Really hot.
And I'm sort of excited for you both
even though –
Yeah.
I don't know?
It's a good thing!
What happened,
isn't it?
The improvisation sort of wound me up
and took over.
And you had said before that um...

(She consults her notebook.)

That we should allow the characters we created to LEAD our improv.
"Don't fear
where the doors your subconscious unlocks with your partner
might lead you..."
And Mistress MacGregor unlocked some doors
let me tell you.
Doors that –
And I
well,

ALANA. I became a woman I've never been before
over there,
you know?
I've never...
I don't know that there has ever been a time
when I've known how to tell a man
what I've wanted or have felt free to follow every embarrassing impulse
I've had
And like...
I don't...
babe?
Was it?
Was it as good for you?
Or did you...

*(***PHILLIP** *nods.)*

PHILLIP. Totally.

ALANA. Exactly!
Yeah.
Our bodies were talking
in ways we haven't been able to...
I mean,
and it's been said so I hope I'm not embarrassing you baby...
but we were able to navigate around some of the issues that
we've been having with
you know...
"E.D."...
not with a pill but with
um...
Well,
our improv...

And...
I just.
I felt a connection.
A real one.
And I honestly feel like.
If I can speak for the group...
I just don't know why we ALL had to stop
because
I honestly feel like
we were getting to a place
as a couple
where if we had been
allowed
to continue?
I feel as though we would've
found a real place of sexual communion
/ and release.

> (**JIM** *lets out a laugh.*)

> (**ALANA** *looks over to him.*)

What's funny?

JIM. Nothing.
Keep going.

PATRICIA. No, Jim
I think,
yeah,
I think you just inserted yourself into Alana's space
of direct and honest communication
because you have something you needed to add.
So please.
Add to the conversation.

...

Don't retreat.

PATRICIA. You know?
   Let's, like
   …
   let's build?
   You know?
   Not tear down.

JIM. …
   …
   …
   …

TEÁ. Jim,
   I think what I'm sensing
   is some…
   and this is completely from my perception
   of how your actions
   are impacting me
   and me alone at this moment,
   but I'm
   yeah,
   I'm sensing some real hostility.
   And something I know from my own training
   is that
   hostility MUST be unpacked
   and processed /
   in order for –

JIM. WHAT THE FUCK DID I SAY ABOUT THE WORD PROCESS?
   This is insane.
   This is insane
   This.
   Is.
   Insane.
   What is going on here?

I don't even know where to begin.
You all
with your
words
and your
this
this
frankly,
this nonsense is making messes
starting fires
where there were none.
This was supposed to be therapy.
Therapy to
help my wife.
And all I'm seeing is / a bunch...

TEÁ. Therapy.
That is what you're seeing:
Antebellum Sexual Performance Therapy.
A RADICAL therapy designed to help black partners re-engage
intimately with white partners from whom they no longer receive sexual pleasure.
A therapy that, like
you
and your wife
signed up for willingly Jim.
And a therapy that YOU,
Jim,
disrupted today
for not only you and Kaneisha,
but for everyone else
here in this room breaching a contract
and partnership you had made with each of the other
people in this room over the last three days.

(A stunned silence.)

PATRICIA. But this is good Jim.
You're articulating.
You're starting to connect to us.
Even if it's through aggression.
Like we said in the packet,
"Aggression is welcomed into the space
as an accelerant to radical breakthroughs."
When aggression is utilized and manipulated / safely and –

JIM. "Utilized and manipulated" you people / are in –

KANEISHA. Jim!
Shut up!
Let them speak.
I –
I –
Let them speak.

>   (**KANEISHA** *breathes. One breath in, one breath out.*)

TEÁ. Kaneisha,
this,
Um,
this like
feels like a moment when you would like to share
your own
experience.
Yet I do feel like we should allow
you know,
like
Jim to have a moment to continue to articulate his feelings
since

he did stop the fantasy play
and obviously felt some sort of trauma that he hasn't completely worked out.
Is that fair, Jim?

JIM. No.
No it's not.
I –
Do not feel that that is fair at all.
I feel like this whole thing
is traumatizing my wife
my relationship.
She's sitting here
like a rock
she's snapping at me
and / I feel –

PHILLIP. Aren't we supposed to be talking about our own feelings?
Not the
um...
The
uh –

GARY. The experiences of others.

DUSTIN. *(Whispered.)* Please stay out of it, Gary.

JIM. I was talking about my experience
My experience of her experience.

GARY. *(To* **DUSTIN***)* / Don't dictate to me.

PHILLIP. But also –
Did he –
/ Did you say Starbucks?

DUSTIN. Well don't dictate to him!
He was saying what he was saying
and you completely interjected into / the co–

TEÁ. Woah
partners!
Hey
Let's all stand up.
Come on.
Stand up.
Let's
yeah
this is
um
something that we learned when we were studying in Ghana last summer.
Come on,
get up.

(They all stand.)

OK,
um so breathe in,
deeply,
OK...
then bend down like me.
Put your head between your legs as best as you can and just:

*(**TEÁ** screams.)*

*(They all look at her uncomfortably, then they do it as well. Except **JIM**, who sort of looks around confused then puts his head between his legs before popping back up, perturbed.)*

PATRICIA. OK.
Great.
You can sit.
Do you all feel a bit...?
Better?

(Some nods.)

JIM. What I was saying was
that
my experience of this whole thing
is
utter confusion.
I feel as though I've stepped into a madhouse
and like you said,
I did so willingly.
I did so because my wife thought that this would help her.
And I don't know how
or why
because you all,
this all
feels so
deeply –
I don't know how we can sit here
and listen as people talk about how "hot"
this was.
…
…
This was not hot.
You made me call my wife a "negress"
a...
She made me call her a "negress."
And that's –
She's my queen.

KANEISHA. *(To herself.)* Oh god.

JIM. It's true.
You are.
And I see all of you
and

JIM. you know
we have you two

   (He points to **ALANA** *and* **PHILLIP**.*)*

Who seem to have been on cloud nine
which I just /
I
I
don't understand.

ALANA. Wow…
OK?

TEÁ. Please keep this centered on you and your experience / Jim.

JIM. And
yes it's amazing that YOU came Gary.
It is.
You came and you enjoyed it.
But it doesn't seem like Dustin did.
Does it?
Anybody?
And I know for a fact that I didn't because there's no way I possibly could.
Everything about this is sickening to me.
It turns my stomach,
and I personally don't find a turnt stomach to be hot.
OR erotic.
OK?
/
That's how I feel.
That's my "unpacking."
That's where I stand with my "processing."

   *(***DUSTIN** *begins to shake his head.)*

ALANA. Is this allowed? /
Is he allowed to speak this way?

DUSTIN. I just want to say,
for the record,
that I was –
yes.
I was upset by a lot of what the improv
or like fantasy play
brought up for us
and about me.
but like
he did come.
You know?
And he hasn't
with me at least
he hasn't in
months?
years?
I think?
But…
yeah my only thing is that like
he got really into it.
And then he cried you know?
Which is confusing.
Fuck!
It wasn't even just a cry
he was shaking,
shivering
you were hyperventilating babe.
You wouldn't let me touch you…
But even then,
we didn't stop it,
I didn't stop it

DUSTIN. you all did.
 He did.
 You stopped the play.
 But like you got SO INTO IT, babe.

GARY. You won't let this up will you?

DUSTIN. No.
 I won't.
 I can't
 I feel
 like
 …
 like this???
 What you made me do today?
 I'm an actor
 OK?
 I said:
 "yes, and…"
 That's it.
 I was letting you lead me down a path
 and it was a dark and scary one but I said "yes, and…"
 because you
 before we started you said,
 "Baby I think I need this. /

GARY. / I know what I said
 I don't… –

DUSTIN. – I think I need you to do this."
 So I did it.
 I've done it.
 But I don't know if what I did
 Is what caused you that release
 or if what I did caused you those tears
 or if it was some fucked up combination of both

but I'm just
yeah...
I don't know what to do with your tears.
You gotta know
that hurts me too babe.
Like I did something.
Like I got too into it?
Or...
yeah.

> (**DUSTIN** *puts his hands on his face. Willing tears not to stream down it.*)

TEÁ. OK.
So that's
yeah
we're getting a lot out.
This,
yeah.
Thank you both.
For sharing that.

> (**PATRICIA** *looks over to* **KANEISHA**, *who is holding on to her sweatpants, plucking at loose strands of cotton.*)

PATRICIA. Kaneisha?
We haven't heard anything from you yet.
How are you feeling?
Right now?
What's your immediate response to what we just saw?

KANEISHA. ...
...
I don't know that I'm fully articulate right now.
I'd rather hear from other voices.
I think that might be the best way to move forward.

KANEISHA. For me.
Right now.
Just.
Yeah.
...
...
I'm feeling a bit betrayed.
Because...
Yeah.
"Starbucks"...
...
The fact that...
The minute I express
what I need from him
How I need it.
He shut down
Made a half step...
Even after all the prep on Day Two and Day Three
he –
I –
...
So I'm trying to come back from that.
Come up for air.
Before I try to
um
before I try to put voice behind my emotions.
Because at this moment I think anything I say will feel thoughtless.

(**JIM** *sits, stunned a bit, shifting uncomfortably. "Betrayed"?*)

PATRICIA. I totally hear that.
Um...

TEÁ. Should we –
I think it's time that we move
to another communication sphere.
For the moment.
How does that sound?
To everyone?

(Everyone shifts uncomfortably.)

PATRICIA. Yes,
I think,
We've heard a lot of things
and I just want to place those things back into the space
as I heard them
so that perhaps each of your respective partners
can hear them
and pro–
RUMINATE

(She laughs.)

on the things you have said from
a space of neutrality.

*(**JIM** begins to furiously rub his face. **KANEISHA** looks over and shifts uncomfortably.)*

*(**PATRICIA** and **TEÁ** exchange a glance and then both begin scrolling up on their iPads.)*

TEÁ. OK, Gary?
...
...
...
GARY. Yes?

TEÁ. OK...
So,
Dustin wanted to put into the space that
you came.
He wanted to articulate that it felt like a mutual accomplishment
because
that is a physical response that he hasn't shared with you
in months.
...
...
He wanted to also express that he felt complicated
about this accomplishment
because you cried.

(**GARY** *sighs.*)

He also felt complicated because
in his words: "you got so into it."
He was trying to parse out if
because of your deep immersion into this psychic space
– the fantasy play –
if he had misjudged
as both a partner
and as an actor
what you needed from him.
He wanted you to know that when you hurt
he was hurt too.
Now it seems – and this is leading –
but now it seems he's trying to figure out if that hurt was the kind of hurt you needed.

GARY. It was.
it.
yeah...

it was.

...

...

...

(**PATRICIA** *nods and looks at her iPad.*)

PATRICIA. Dustin?

DUSTIN. Yes?

PATRICIA. *(Reading.)* Dustin...
Gary,
um,
Gary agreed with you that
he did indeed come.
He said that he liked it
he enjoyed it.
He said that he felt like
you didn't like the experience
or had
some complications with it
because you didn't like having to be
"white."
But most importantly,
Gary said multiple times that he enjoyed the fact that
he met one of his personal goals for this experience...
He came.

(**DUSTIN** *looks to* **GARY**, *who isn't looking at him.*)

DUSTIN. I feel / like...

TEÁ. I think before we have responses
we should continue placing back into the room all the things
that have been articulated.
So that everyone hears.

DUSTIN. I –

...

...

TEÁ. Next,
um
we heard from Alana.

...

Phillip?

PHILLIP. Yes.

TEÁ. Alana expressed
that,
for her,
the experience was
"Just hot."
She said that the improvisation
sort of wound her up.
That it took her over
and that she became a woman she's never been before
in the fantasy play.
Alana felt that you and she had a real connection.
That you two were getting to a place of
"sexual communion."
She expressed she feels that
if the fantasy play hadn't been halted
then you would have gotten
somewhere very healthy for the both of you.

PHILLIP. OK.

ALANA. And yeah...
I also just –
I think I would've said more / had I not –

PATRICIA. We know.
There's plenty of time Alana.

But OK,
Alana?

ALANA. Yes?

PATRICIA. *(Scrolling up and down her iPad.)* OK...
Alana,
Phillip agreed with you.
Phillip felt like he too thought it was
"totally" hot.

> *(A silence. For a few moments.)*

TEÁ. OK...
Kaneisha?

KANEISHA. Uh-huh?

TEÁ. Kaneisha,
Jim feels...
that this whole thing is insane.
He feels as though we are starting fires
where there weren't any before
and he also feels like he sees you Kaneisha
in a state that is – to articulate in my own words –
a state that is foreign to him at this moment.

> *(**JIM** places a hand on **KANEISHA**'s thigh, palm up, as though waiting for her to place hers in his as well.)*

> *(**KANEISHA** looks at **TEÁ**. Her hand does not move.)*

Jim feels as though
what has transpired today is inflicting trauma
on not only you, Kaneisha,
but also on your relationship.
He doesn't understand what is to be accomplished by him,

TEÁ. in his words,
>having to call his wife a "negress" when you, Kaneisha, are a queen to him.
>Everything about this day has turned his stomach.
>…
>…
>…

PATRICIA. Jim?

JIM. Yes?

PATRICIA. Kaneisha feels as though she can't articulate much at this moment.
>But she does feel betrayed.

>*(Silence.)*

>*(**JIM** moves his hand.)*

KANEISHA. …
>…
>betrayed might be –
>I –
>…
>…
>yeah.

TEÁ. It's OK Kaneisha.
>It's –
>everything is OK, everybody.
>This is good.
>This is just where we are right now.
>At this moment.

>*(**PATRICIA** stands up and turns off her iPad. She has a bit of an excited smile that she is attempting to swallow back as it grows.)*

PATRICIA. Now,
I'd love to just have someone
say to the room,
what they feel they understood
from what we just read.

(**ALANA** *raises her hand.*)

TEÁ. Alana?

ALANA. I noticed.
That it's sort of startling that
the words that seemed the most at the forefront
of the discourse were those of the
white men in the room.
Which / for me was j–

DUSTIN. I'm not white!
I said that Day One!
I'm not
white!
I'm not.
Please, don't fucking say that.
It's ignorant.
It's erasure and it's –
that's…
that's
fucking violent.
And so casual!
A white woman being casually violent,
who would've guessed it!

PHILLIP. / Hey!

DUSTIN. That's the sort of thing

(*He looks to* **GARY.**)

DUSTIN. You say you deal with shit
that it's overwhelming
that you can't take it
that you feel like you're drowning every day?
That's what you're saying at home all the time...
Well this is what the fuck I get.
Every single day
a fucking erasure.
By her.
By him.
By them.
And by you.

GARY. Dustin,
Ha!
I don't even –
No one is erasing / you.

DUSTIN. When our lease ran out and I wanted to move you / said –

GARY. You still care about that?
/ You –

DUSTIN. Yes!
I do still care
because
when I said that I wanted to move to a nicer area
the argument that flared up
around your PERCEPTION that
that meant a "whiter" neighborhood completely
disregarded the fact that
for me
the world isn't black or white...

GARY. OK so we're pulling out that file?
Here?

DUSTIN. Yes
 Yes we are because
 there are shades in between
 and perhaps the reason I don't want to live
 in East Harlem anymore
 has nothing to do with me not wanting to
 live near black people
 and has everything to do with me wanting to be able to get to an audition
 on time
 without having to walk almost a mile to get to a decent train.
 I live with a black person every day
 that's not the issue.
 If anything the issue is that
 living where we live
 I'm forced to be just another white gentrifier to my neighbors.
 An intruder...
 Which just isn't true...
 you're the one who's constantly bathing in every comfort gentrification
 has to offer in neighborhood.
 But I'm the "white" one...
 and
 No one knows or cares
 or –

 (The tears start to stream.)

 *(**ALANA** looks over as though she wants to comfort him or do something.)*

TEÁ. OK let it flow.
 In this space
 A tearless face is just a mask.

ALANA. *(To no one in particular.)* / I'm sorry I wasn't trying to...
I wasn't even really talking about him I –

PATRICIA. Exactly
this is not a place for masks
and a lot of masks
the ones we hold up on and over our faces
every day are starting to come off.
And they are heavy.
And when you let that much weight go
a lot of shit comes with it
there are side effects.

    (Turning to **DUSTIN**.*)*

And I just want to say to you
I –
I understand as a person
who identifies with,
has wrestled with
and who recognizes their own brownness that
this type of work can feel erasing.
Emphasis on feel.
But I can also say that that is a logic of white supremacy.
On Day One when we self-identified
we attempted to foster an open dialogue
around the spectrum of racial identity
but once we began in earnest
we clearly stated that the work we were doing to aid
the black partners in these relationships
benefits from a recognition of not how we see ourselves
but how the world
and by extension
they see those of us here

who are not black-identified but exist
somewhere on that spectrum
closer to white than black.

>   (**DUSTIN** *just stares at* **PATRICIA**.)

>   (**GARY** *stares at* **DUSTIN**.)

PHILLIP. All this feels like bullshit to me.

TEÁ. Why is that Phillip?

PHILLIP. It,
> like,
> It just does.
> I don't.
> Yeah…

>   (*There's a long pause as everyone waits for him to speak.*)

ALANA. I think what he's saying
> is that
> baby tell me if I'm off base…
> but that
> You all
> You gave us clear instructions about
> what this therapy was going to be
> you said:
> "Antebellum Sexual Performance Therapy is going to require you
> to be with your partners
> in ways that may scare
> or trigger
> you and your partner"
> you know?
> blah blah blah.
> You said it was going to be hard.

ALANA. And it was
   but it's frustrating having these fights
   right now
   about what did or didn't happen
   who feels what way or not
   when for some reason
   not even halfway through our day
   the rug ripped from beneath us
   and all this work we'd done
   preparing for Day Four
   got...
   just...

   (Starting to cry.)

   And some of us just feel like
   we...
   We just wanted to keep doing the work.

DUSTIN. I –

PHILLIP. That,
   yeah...

PATRICIA. OK,
   I think this is a good place to reorient and refocus
   on what brought us here:
   Tackling anhedonia at its source.

TEÁ. Yes,
   this therapy,
   Antebellum Sexual Performance Therapy,
   this process,
   has been shaped by the two of us
   first at Smith, then at Yale University
   over the last five years.

   *(**TEÁ** stands up and joins **PATRICIA**.)*

PATRICIA. I think it's important that we examine and name
the dynamic that Alana pointed out a bit ago:
In the aftermath of confronting
and dissecting racial trauma
the people in the room who were the
first to verbalize their experience
of the trauma's confrontation
were those who have the closest proximity
to white supremacy.

> *(Pause.)*
>
> *(***PATRICIA** *looks around the room and lets her statement live within it.)*

TEÁ. So in a sense,
Alana was exactly right.

PATRICIA. Yes,
but also somewhat myopic because
Alana, you didn't see how you yourself
also took up space that your partner didn't at all.

TEÁ. A lot of the / work we've –

PATRICIA. *(To* **ALANA***.)* And that myopia,
that positionality
that places a black partner
squarely in the blind
spot of their nonblack partner
is a myopia I've had
and am still actively dismantling
through the work Teá and I developed as our relationship began
to find itself at impasses of communication and empathy
about four years ago.

(This moves through the room...)

(So **TEÁ** *and* **PATRICIA** *are also a couple...)*

(A warmth passes between them and a new energy takes over the room.)

TEÁ. A lot of the work
we are doing
and
have been doing
is about shining a light on these dynamics
in order to radically center the black body
in discourses around white supremacy.
A major aspect of both this therapy
and our research
are the ways in which racialized trauma
has not only transfigured the modes
by which minoritarian individuals
conceive of self
but also the mode by which the
minoritarian conceives self
in relation to the other.

PATRICIA. Watching the dynamics
that just unfolded in this
group – uh –
"rumination"
coincided with so much of the work
we have been doing in our thesis.

TEÁ. Completely.
It's incredibly exciting.
And while today, in many ways,
the breakthroughs or the "goals" we were hoping to reach
this week through our Day Four fantasy play

were derailed...
I must say the unpacking that's taken place here
will have a SIGNIFICANT impact on our research.
This is unparalleled.

PATRICIA. The goal of a lot of this work
has been in proving
for not only us but for you all
that your inability to feel things sexually,
your anhedonia,
is directly related to
the fact that black and brown people
after generations of subjugation,
raping,
pillaging,
now only nurture and birth children
who are neurologically atypical
and undiagnosed.
We know this because we watched it manifest in our own relationship
and have been studying it
in the relationships of countless others
as our research has matured and grown
as most of you read in the most recent swelling of press around this work.

TEÁ. Yes.
As you read there:
The black or brown subject
born under the constant psychological warfare
of the white supremacist, heteropatriarchal,
capitalist system
has been stricken
with disorders that have gone unrecognized
because there is no racial

TEÁ. or social lens
on the psyche in our current deeply
conservative practice of psychology and psychoanalysis.
And like,
that's scary you know?
To realize that like
even with all the big work we have to do in the macro
systemically
there's even bigger work
but in the micro of the mind
that isn't being done at all.

PHILLIP. I'm confused.
So,
like,
are you saying that my –
um –
The reason I can't get it up.
The reason I don't come
is because of –
just like,
racism?

TEÁ. Well,
in a sense,
yes.
But more so,
that the reason you, Gary,
and Kaneisha
were chosen for this therapy
was because you each
showed the most pronounced
symptoms of
what we're calling
in our forthcoming book:

"Racialized Inhibiting Disorder"
or RID.

GARY. And what are the symptoms?

PATRICIA. Well we just saw one of the most pronounced,
Alexithymia

JIM. Alexi-what?

KANEISHA. Alexithymia is the inability to
describe your own feelings.

TEÁ. *(Surprised.)* Exactly...
and while many of you are quite adept at this in certain spaces
I mean,
you're a writer Kaneisha,
so obviously you can articulate feelings on or about things,
yet in this instance we saw it
manifest itself in the way we recognize it most in those with RID:
None of you were able to
articulate or locate articulation
for your state in the aftermath of our
fantasy play with race-based trauma.
We first came upon this in our own lives when we
realized that many of the traumas I was experiencing
and Patricia was witnessing me experience during our time at Yale
had affected our relationship dynamics in ways I couldn't name.

PATRICIA. And because much of my focus has been in
cognitive psychology
and epigenetics we began to tease out an understanding of what was happening between us
first using the language of psychology and then

PATRICIA. turning outward towards black feminist theory
and queer theory which is much of Teá's focus.
We began cataloguing other anxiety disorders
that we theorized compounded to
to create in Teá and
many of our subjects,
including you three,
the anhedonia you all are suffering from,
that include:
panic attacks (which I think you experienced at the end of your fantasy play Gary),
social anxiety,
and most pronounced in each of you
Obsessive Compulsive Disorder
with acute musical obsession disorder.

TEÁ. Which is one of the reasons
this therapy
is situated around prolonged exposure
via Antebellum Sexual Performance Therapy to
engage with the concerns
that you have raised
Jim.

(Silence.)

PATRICIA. I know.
This is a lot.

TEÁ. And like,
where we are moving now.
Now that we have
like
laid out the framework for our thinking
we are
well

we would like
to dive deep into
more questions
primarily to the three of you
who have been
relatively silent
to try to
manuever around your alexithymia
so you can hear yourself
name your feelings
in order to get to a similar place of materiality
with your emotions
free of the fantasy play
or the trauma that illicited said materiality.

PATRICIA. But Teá…
before we begin to
go down that rabbit hole
I feel like we just dumped a lot of information in their laps…
so –
I want to have a moment
to just hear your questions.
Your challenges with our methodology,
if any,
before we move on.

TEÁ. Thank you Patricia…
you're right.
…
…
We want to make sure
we are giving everyone a chance
to take the floor.
In the ways they feel most comfortable.

*(Hands go up. Everyone but **JIM** and **KANEISHA** seem to have questions.)*

PATRICIA. Yes Phillip?

PHILLIP. So,
   yeah,
   Like I don't really have a question per se…
   Just like,
   ummmmmmm,
   OK so like
   I don't know like half the words you just said.
   It,
   yeah to me
   it all sounds kind of
   …
   …
   like –
   OK,
   Ale-xyyy-thImia?

TEÁ. Alexithymia.

PHILLIP. Yes.
   That.
   What makes you think any of us actually have that
   or that it's specific
   to us at all?
   You know?
   Because I'm just thinking back
   to like, some of the like
   some of the girlfriends I've had like
   couldn't even
   like they didn't even have the ability to like
   call me "black"
   Or even see me as black.

And like
the thing about people who are close to
like white privilege or whatever?
I mean I'm pretty close.
I mean I'm not white.
But I feel like
people have to will me black
for me to be black
otherwise
I'm just a sort of
like
Just a hot guy who's not exactly black
or white.
…
…
I don't know?
I guess
I'm just
I'm remembering
that
like so in college
I was
—
I went to a really white school
like the whitest
a good school
Wake Forest?
you know?
Division One soccer.
And like
I was a freshman
but I was good
and like

PHILLIP. I remember
　like
　one time I was kicking this little white boy's ass during a scrimmage
　and when we went back
　after
　like after the scrimmage or whatever
　we went back and like…
　we were showering and
　that white kid was like
　"look at donkey dick over there
　I always forget Phillip's a nigger
　till I see that thing swinging
　because he definitely doesn't play soccer like a nigger"
　…
　…
　And like I don't know
　yeah…
　I can't remember his name but this upperclassman
　like looked over and was like
　"Phillip isn't a nigger Phillip's Phillip."
　and yeah
　I think,
　that that's basically what everyone thinks of me.
　I'm not black
　I'm not white
　I'm just Phillip.
　And Phillip's like this
　superhuman dude
　who's beyond,
　like,
　black and white.
　You know?

So I'm just
yeah
I'm confused why I would have
this inability to like
say how I feel about
racial trauma?
Because at this time
I don't have any
like

...

I have no memories
of being traumatized
more than like...
I don't know?
or even to the same like...

...

...

Yeah,
to the same scale as some of the other people here?
Does that?
That doesn't make sense does it?

TEÁ. No,
It does.
It completely does
as a fair-skinned black woman
it makes perfect sense to me
that there would be reticence about owning
your traumas
or being able to point to them as such.
Yet, I want to assure you that
you wouldn't be here if we hadn't located
traumas in your briefing interviews
that we perceived as race-based.

TEÁ. ...
> ...
> I also want to say I'm sorry.
> What happened in that locker room
> was...
> yeah.
> I want you to know that I see you.
> Do you mind if we leave that question in the room
> and come back to it later?

>> (**JIM** *raises his hand.*)

JIM. Can I go to the restroom?

PATRICIA. Ummm...
> well.

TEÁ. Yes, Jim.
> No one is keeping you in the room.

JIM. Thank you.

>> (**JIM** *exits.*)

>> (*Other hands are still raised.*)

TEÁ. Yes Gary?

GARY. I think,
> yeah
> I think I'm just confused
> about the
> musical obsession disorder?
> What is that?
> Is that why you played that
> music during our fantasy play?

>> (**PATRICIA** *looks at* **TEÁ** *knowingly.*)

DUSTIN. What music?

GARY. The like,
  the song…
  the song that was playing when we started wrestling,
  right before we…

DUSTIN. There wasn't a song playing.

GARY. I –

TEÁ. So OK…
  We usually talk about this later
  but um
  the music you heard Gary
  what
  was it?

GARY. The music?
  "Multi-Love"?

TEÁ. OK.
  And do you hear that song very often?

GARY. I guess?
  It um,
  yeah…
  it gets stuck in my head a lot.

PATRICIA. How much is a lot?
  Once a day?
  Twice a day?

GARY. Like all day?

PATRICIA. You constantly hear it?

GARY. Not constantly
  but…
  yeah…
  a lot I guess?
  It um –

GARY. I know it
   because they play it at the coffee shop
   Down from our house
   where I'm –
   where I go sometimes.

PATRICIA. And did you hear it constantly while you were doing fantasy play?

GARY. ...
   ...
   ...
   um,
   well...
   I guess.
   No?
   Only the once.

KANEISHA. *(To* **PATRICIA.***)* That's an OCD thing right?

GARY. What is?

KANEISHA. Sometimes
   when people have OCD
   when they do a more strenuous mental task
   they don't find themselves
   stricken with
   whatever it is that causes them anxiety usually.

TEÁ. Yes,
   exactly.

KANEISHA. I um
   I was diagnosed with OCD
   when I was in middle school.
   One of my teachers was really concerned
   because
   I would um,
   I would have panic attacks

or like something like it
something like a mini panic attack?
When she wouldn't erase the board all the way.
I'd start to like shake
and stuff.
It was,
yeah...
And there was this one teacher
who didn't care? You know
Who
she would say
"Oh don't worry bout Kaneisha
she just a little flicted"
Which I guess meant afflicted?
I don't...
But Mrs. Wright she told my parents I should um
I should get a therapist.
My parents didn't believe in therapy
though.
So...
Anyway...
I googled a lot.
Made sense of it myself.

(**KANEISHA** *looks down, a bit embarrassed.*)

TEÁ. Thank you for sharing that Kaneisha.

GARY. ...

...
But it
like
it didn't sound the way it normally does
it was like
it was amplified or something?
I'm not sure.

PATRICIA. That was the therapy.
　You were getting to a very raw place
　if you felt as though
　it was…
　…
　…
　with exposure
　there is an intensification
　of all the symptoms of RID
　that build to a place of
　hopefully
　a sort of release and freedom from those same symptoms
　in order to get us to some place of
　stasis
　or neutrality.

>　　(**JIM** *walks back into the room, his hands in his pockets, and quietly sits back in his seat.*)

ALANA. *(Her hand raised.)* Um…
　…
　I just –
　I was going to ask something else
　but I
　…
　Phillip do you have this
　um
　Musical obsessive disorder
　or –
　What do you hear?

PHILLIP. …

PATRICIA. He plays through it,
　but compulsively.
　Right, Phillip?

PHILLIP. You mean the Beethoven?

PATRICIA. How often do you play that?

PHILLIP. Um...
Like every day?

PATRICIA. How many times?
Always the fourth movement?

PHILLIP. I can't even –

ALANA. Wow.
Wow, yeah he's –
yeah...
wow.

(**KANEISHA** *raises her hand.*)

TEÁ. Kaneisha?

KANEISHA. Are you still going to ask us questions?

TEÁ. Would you like us to ask you questions?

KANEISHA. Yes.
I think I would yes.

TEÁ. Why?

KANEISHA. Why?
...
um...
...
...
Well because I feel as though
I –
I feel that I haven't used my voice enough.
I feel that I want to scream
and I've already done that so I'd rather just speak.
I feel like I
as though

KANEISHA. constantly
subterfuge
is the engine of my subconscious
as though
It's constantly driving the vehicle of my psyche
and so I'm never sure that
I'm truly in control
and earlier today
when we were in fantasy play
I finally felt in control
of that engine.
I felt in control.
Until.
Until everything stopped.

>   (**KANEISHA** *looks to* **JIM**.)

>   (**JIM** *looks down*.)

TEÁ. That's –
thank you
Kaneisha.
That's beautiful.
All of it.
Who else felt in control?

GARY. I did.
I think that my experience
very much aligns with yours
um
Kaneisa?

KANEISHA. Kaneisha.

PHILLIP. Mine didn't.

PATRICIA. It didn't?

>   (**ALANA** *looks over, concerned*.)

PHILLIP. No, not
   yeah
   I can't say that I felt
   in control
   at all.
   I mean...
   yeah I definitely didn't.
   I felt like
   I felt like a slave.
   Literally.
   I think.
   Yeah I went deep into it.
   And I think that
   I felt
   sort of like
   I mean
   ...
   Baby
   It was hot,
   don't get me wrong.
   But like
   ...
   ...
   it's not that different from dynamics we've had in the bedroom.

ALANA. What?

   (She starts to laugh.)

   What are you talking about Phillip?
   That –
   we've never done anything like that.

PHILLIP. We met on FetLife.

DUSTIN. FetLife?

JIM. It's like Tinder for fetish fiends.

PHILLIP. Yes.

ALANA. Yes,
> but I wasn't
> we weren't doing ANYTHING like this.

PHILLIP. Your husband had a cucking
> fantasy.

ALANA. Yeah and?

PHILLIP. I mean...
> I didn't
> I wasn't thinking about it at the time
> but
> yeah...
> I felt like the little nigger boy
> You all had invited into the house
> to dick you down while he watched in the chair beside us.
> While you told him he had a little "wee thing."
> That / didn't feel –

ALANA. That had NOTHING to do with race.
> That was just what got him off
> that was just...
> that was just his way of...

PHILLIP. / Baby baby, don't freak out I know it felt more complicated for you...

> (**PHILLIP** and **ALANA** *continue to whisper argue.*)

ALANA. (*Sotto voce.*) / But that...that had nothing to do with me
> with us.
> Today was about you.
> About us.

I –
I –

DUSTIN. I'm sorry I feel like an idiot but
um
what's cucking?

KANEISHA. It's when a white man wants to get off
watching a black man fuck his
white wife.

ALANA. It wasn't racial.
I swear it wasn't.

KANEISHA. Maybe not for you.

PHILLIP. *(A lot is at the surface of this.)* It was for me…
fuck!
Woah…
Fuck.
Yeah…
And it DEFINITELY was for him too.
And it was fine
because
I liked it.
I almost liked that more.
Maybe that's why my dick worked more.
Maybe my dick only works
when I know I'm black.
And it doesn't know I'm black
when I'm fucking you
because you love me too much
you see me too –
Phillip!
You see me
too Phillip!
for you

PHILLIP. this fantasy
  can just be
  fantasy
  but for your husband
  fuck.
  ...
  damn.
  ...
  How am I just hearing myself think this?
  ...
  ...
  But like
  Maybe for Jonathan
  when I was –
  when he was watching me on you
  I could feel his eyes
  seeing me as a nigger
  the big ol nigger
  on his wife
  on you
  and not
  as like
  "Phillip"?
  You know?
  And
  maybe my dick
  likes
  LIKED
  the idea that I'd finally been forced
  into some sort of space where
  it knew how it was being desired
  ...
  ...Yeah...
  does that make sense?

(**PHILLIP** *is obviously emotional but swallowing it all.*)

ALANA. *(Tears start slowly but build.)* Oh baby,
oh…
Listen
look at me
we're going to figure this out.
We –
I left him for a reason.
I
maybe this doesn't help
but I want you to just be my Phillip
my wonderfully
complex and beautiful man
…
…
you are.
I don't
Maybe I'm making things worse.
But –
yeah.
Am I even supposed to be talking?
I –
you said that you –
that –
um?
you said only the black people were supposed to be in control on Day Four.
Did –
Did I mess up?
I tried to do everything you said
right.
I just –
I wanted to help him.

ALANA. Did.
>Did I...did I not give
>him enough space to um...?
>I just –
>This doesn't feel right this doesn't feel.
>Is this even a real study?
>Is this even –

>>(**ALANA** *stands up and begins to shake.*)

>>(*She bends down and does the screaming thing that they all did before.*)

TEÁ. We're all processing
>This is all good.
>This is getting to the good place.

DUSTIN. I think
>if we are all processing
>I very much want to process
>this,
>the why
>of all of this
>because...
>...
>I'm not trying to say that like
>I'm more oppressed
>by like
>white supremacy
>or something
>but I'm
>I've
>I've
>very much felt like
>traumatized
>by it.

Deeply.
Even today
I've felt like
so many little
nicks
and cuts
in every moment of this whole
therapy
and I...
Like is there even any room for me in this?
like...
yeah I'm happy that THEY feel that
you have
some sort of
like
ownership of the racial dynamics in our sex life
Gary but I don't know man...
this is just.
I'm not white.
I can't be white
and I still don't understand how your idea of my "whiteness"
is what you need me to acknowledge to / be –

GARY. You always say you're not white
but what are you?

DUSTIN. What?

GARY. What are you
if you're not white
because you never say...
you just
you get to exist in this place of "non-whiteness."

DUSTIN. You know I'm not white.
You know what the fuck I am.

GARY. Well sometimes I forget
and need to be reminded.
Need you to really lay out for me the ways
that you being confused for "white"
is anywhere near as traumatizing for you
as my growing up without a choice to be anything but –
because I'm black
black black
blue black
jet black
raisin black
eerie black
people have seen so much color in me they could make
a new rainbow with the shades but they always go back
to black.
Because even with all the shades
they still call me black.
Now I could call you
off-white
dark white
eggshell!
But every time I still go back to white with you.
So what are you, if not white?

DUSTIN. I'm not going to dignify that with / any sort –

GARY. Dignify that?
Dignify me!
With just one fucking ATTEMPT AT –!

(GARY kicks a chair with a scream.)

(PATRICIA stands up excitedly.)

PATRICIA. You know what?
I think this is a moment, where
it's time to use aggression

as an accelerant to your progress.
There's a lot repressed here
between the two of you
and I think
it's important that now we make space for you
to unlock some of the anger and aggression with which you've had
a push-pull relationship to
this entire process.
So Gary
since you've had less space
to take the floor
and that was one of your goals
I want you to speak…
don't feel stifled by niceties.
Speak from the aggressive place
because that feels to be one of the ways that you two know how to move forward.
It worked in your fantasy play
let's see if it works here.

>   (**PATRICIA** *takes a step back, and* **TEÁ** *pulls out her iPad and begins taking more notes.*)
>
>   (**GARY** *stares at* **DUSTIN**. **DUSTIN** *stares back.*)

GARY. …

   …
   …
   …

DUSTIN. …
   She said speak.

GARY. From aggression.
   She said speak from aggression.
   And I've expelled

GARY. all of it.
I'm done.
To speak to you from aggression
would mean to speak to you like I care.
And I don't.
I don't give a fuck anymore.
I don't even know if I like you.
I just know that whatever love I have for you
is the only reason I'm even talking
to you right now.
Because I just want to crawl into myself and disappear
for a good little while.
I feel stupid.
"I refuse to dignify that."
How dare you?
"I refuse to dignify that"
I'm so fucking stupid.
So
fucking
stupid.
For almost a decade I've given myself over
to someone who doesn't dignify me
who acts like he's the prize
and I'm the lucky recipient.
No motherfucker I'm the prize.
Always have been, always will be.
Somehow I forgot that.
Or I never knew that.
How could I?
Got so wrapped in you
so wrapped up in your presentation.
That I forgot myself
because when someone presents themselves as a prize

you receive them as such.
And when we met
nobody but my mama had ever told me I was a prize
And nobody had ever
thought I deserved to receive one.
But then one day there you were
on the train.
Your little beige belly poking out
and your eyes staring at me from behind a script
like you were saying:
"this is a gift just for you if you're willing to take it"
and I did.
And I loved it.
Because we were babies.
And receiving your gift felt like
a type of reciprocation
like you were receiving me as a gift too.
But you weren't.
You never did.

DUSTIN. / Hey don't say that, why are you saying this?

GARY. I was a comfort object,
a placeholder,
a –
a tool by which your difference could finally be seen.
…
…
right?
Wasn't I?
I think that's what's been at the bottom of all this today.
I finally got to come again because I
was,
finally,
treated like a prize.

GARY. And you,
>you can't –
>your difference from him
>or her
>is no longer allowed to be defined by your proximity to me.
>And you can't stand that.
>Because that's all I was worth to you.
>That's why you don't need to dignify me.
>Because here I don't have any worth to you.
>And now that I know that.
>…
>…
>I don't think you have any worth to me either.

>>*(Suddenly, **DUSTIN** is up and pushing **GARY**. Who isn't pushing back.)*

DUSTIN. What the fuck does that mean?
>Huh?
>What does that mean?
>What are you saying?
>SPEAK!
>SHE SAID SPEAK!
>SPEAK WITH AGGRESSION!
>WITH AGGRESSION!
>HELP US ACCELERATE TO PROGRESS OR WHATEVER
>THE FUCK SHE SAID!

>>*(**PATRICIA** and **TEÁ** drop their iPads, rush over, and seperate the two of them.)*

TEÁ. PARTNERS!
>Woah!
>Woah…

OK.
Let's take a breath.
...
...
...
A lot was said just then...
a lot was said
but I think we should have a moment
where we don't speak directly to each other.
Where we / just –

JIM. I wrote something!
When I was in the bathroom.
That.
Yeah...that
I think... I just
Can I read it...
or?

PATRICIA. Jim...
Please / we are trying to...

(*JIM stands up and pulls out his cell phone, begins to read over PATRICIA.*)

JIM. "Kaneisha,
I'm not you.
Words are not my strong suit.
Words are not my passion.
Words are not how I understand the world.
I recognize that.
I see that.
I love that you love words.
That you use them like glasses to make the world make more sense –
unblur its sharp edges.

JIM. But the words you are now asking me to use
make me see the world in a way that I do not find helpful.
In a way that I find deeply destructive.
Counter-intuitive to my own well-being
even
as you say
they are making you more comfortable
in my
–
In
my presence.
Kaneisha
I am someone who sees.
This is how I navigate the world.
The world is not blurry to me
I don't need to make sense of it with words
because the world shows me who it is
and I see it.
I capture what I see.
I retain it.
Yet,
the last month with you
all I have seen is you looking
at me
as though I were some type of virus.
As though my presence is sickening.
As though the love you once had for me has mutated.
And I don't know what to do with that.
I don't know if I should begin mourning
and move on,
if I should fight and find a way to stay.
Or if I should write a letter every day

showing you in words what it is I see
so that you won't need to make sense of it
with words that do not represent us."

    (**JIM** *lowers the phone and looks at* **KANEISHA**.)

TEÁ. ...

  ...

JIM. ...

  ...

PATRICIA. Jim now that you've gotten that out.
I think it's important
that you attempt to / re-engage with the program –

KANEISHA. *(To herself.)* You're a virus.

TEÁ. Kaneisha...we aren't talking directly to our / partners.

JIM. What?

KANEISHA. *(Laughing.)* You're a virus!
That's –
hahaha.
That's why –
You're THE virus.
(To **JIM**.*)* Baby,
do you know
when you lie on top of me now
all I see is the sickness you carry within you.
And I don't know if I can unlearn that.
Virus!
Baby,
I...
I didn't have a word,
I thought...they said RID.
And I thought that was it

KANEISHA. before
but VIRUS.
It's so simple.
So good.
Virus.
You're a virus.
You're THE virus.

(*Pointing to* **ALANA.**)

You know what Alana?
You were right.
They got it wrong.
They got it so so so wrong.
This is a real study
but these girls don't know half of what they're / talking about.

PATRICIA.	**TEÁ.**
Kaneisha I know a lot has happened today. And you're in a raw place but please engage.	I've given multiple opportunities for our methodologies to be challenged.
	But this is not the way that one does that.
	This is not the way!
	We are scientists!

KANEISHA. (*To* **JIM.**) There's no way
now
I can unknow
as you wipe your
dick
across my lips
that when your people landed on this land
a third of the indigenous population of the entire continent died of disease.

Not disease you actively gave them.
Your mere presence was biological warfare.
VIRUS.
You're a virus.
You're the virus
That's why I look at you as such.
That's why
I –
...
It's a not a pathogen, some UNDIAGNOSED
UNDIAGNOSABLE thing in ME.
It's an undiagnosed, undiagnosable thing in you
and you...and
And
And
And
and –

> (*Suddenly, from above, Rihanna's "Work" begins to play.*)
>
> (**KANEISHA** *puts her hands over her ears.*)

AHHHHHHH!!!!

> (*Everyone moves toward* **KANEISHA** *as:*)

End of Act II

ACT III

"Exorcise"

(Lights fade up on a modern bedroom somewhere in the bowels of the MacGregor Plantation.)

(The song "Work" by Rihanna plays on repeat from above as the evening light of Virginia dances through the window and onto the bed where **KANEISHA** *is lying in between two opened suitcases with clothes spilling in and out of them.)*

(There is a knock at the door.)

(And another.)

KANEISHA. *(Not moving.)* Yes?

(The door opens slightly.)

JIM. *(From behind the door.)* Can, um...
can I come in?

KANEISHA. ...
...
...
do what you wanna do.

*(**JIM** walks in. He looks from the bags to her.)*

(He sees the chair next to the bed.)

>   *(He sits. Silently.)*
>
>   *(They are here for a while.)*
>
>   (**KANEISHA** *sits up and looks at him.*)

KANEISHA. What do you want?

JIM. …

   …

   …

KANEISHA. Jim?

JIM. I think I've said all I can say today.
I just want to listen.
I'm going to sit here
and listen.
Whether you're speaking or not.
I'm going to listen.

KANEISHA. …

JIM. …

>   (**KANEISHA** *gets up from the bed and begins to pack.*)

Wasn't that what all this was about?
Us learning to listen to each other better?

KANEISHA. No.
No it wasn't
it was about you listening to me.
Listening to me
and my body
and what I need,
what it needs.
That's what this was about.
Not

...
...
"listening to each other"
always feels like it's just
listening to you with
asides from me.

JIM. That's not fair.

KANEISHA. Like that!
I'm tired of you dictating what is and isn't fair.
Can't you just take my word on it being fair to me?
Can't you just listen
before defending?
Before you start telling me
why my feelings are not fair to you?
That's –
that,
that...
fuck.
I can't, um...
I can't think straight.
Too much going on
in my head
too much
for me to make sense of
you
and me and you.
And, fuck.

> (**KANEISHA** *sits back down and holds her head.*)
>
> (**JIM** *slides onto the bed and grabs her hand and begins massaging and squeezing her palm and the top of her hand tightly.*)

*("Work" decreases in volume. **JIM** squeezes harder.)*

*(**KANEISHA** looks at **JIM**.)*

KANEISHA. I meant it.
When I said it,
"you're a virus"
I've been trying for...
God!
For the last three years.
To figure out what this feeling
brewing
within me
this sort of fog
that's been blurring your face
revealing you
for a moment
before obscuring you
for three years
I've sat
wondering
what it was.
And it was the virus
your virus.
You aggravate my –
my OCD
I know that
...
I knew that
before they
even –
...
...

they didn't have to tell me
...
...
I wonder when I contracted it?
I –

    (**JIM** *keeps massaging her hand.*)

    (Harder.)

I remember how you looked at me
that night
at the bar
when we first met
how it felt
when I first tasted your eyes on me
because your eyes had a taste
(maybe that was the virus?)
your eyes tasted dry but rich
like my favorite
Chardonnay.
The Kongsgaard?
Do you remember
how that was my nickname for you back then?
Kongsgaard?
It –
yeah...
That's why.
Did I ever...
I never told you that did I?
I...
yeah,
maybe that was where I first
contracted
the virus

KANEISHA. your virus
   as I tasted your eyes
   devouring my smile from across that bar
   on Orchard.
   …
   …
   …
   But it was probably when you opened your mouth
   because
   that
   yeah…
   when you said,
   "not to be terribly rude…"
   and you were so Oxbridge
   so…
   so foreign!
   And I –
   my gut sort of fell
   into my vagina
   or something
   I felt like
   my lower half engorge
   with your,
   "not to be terribly rude."
   I didn't –
   I had never really been with a white man
   before you.
   …
   …
   You know I used to take field trips
   to plantations?
   We never came to the MacGregor
   but every child

who grows up in Virginia
they get a plantation tour.
Three, Four, Five.
"They're fun,
ain't they fun Kaneisha?"
I remember they said that to me
when I was little.
The only black girl
and I would wear the same uniform
to every plantation field trip
...
...
my mama would put these little
pink and blue ribbons in my hair
on my pigtailed cornrows
and I'd wear this white dress
and she'd say
"You wear this with your head held high today
because you want to look proud
for your elders
you want them
seeing you
walking through the devil's house
unafraid of the demons that live in the walls.
You wear this with your head held high
and they'll come out and hold your hand
so none of the greasy-haired,
Wild-eyed children of them demons
will come pawing at you
in front of them.
Don't let yourself be disgraced in front of the elders
they've already suffered enough."
And when I'd walk through

KANEISHA. whenever we were there
>I'd always feel
>the little tingle
>in the back of my neck
>that bit of electricity
>telling me they wanted to hold my hand
>and protect me from the demons
>in the walls
>and in the ground.
>And because I would walk
>with two hands out
>smiling
>and looking up at elders
>nobody else could see
>the wild-eyed
>greasy-haired children of the demons
>who were also on the class trip with me stayed away
>so I never had those formative moments of
>making out beneath the lynching tree
>or being fingered behind the cotton gin
>like the other girls did
>in sixth and seventh grade.
>And never felt a need to
>be touched by a white boy
>
>...
>
>...
>
>till you.
>You were different
>so
>foreign.
>Unamerican.
>Not a demon.
>
>...

...
But you do still have the virus.

> (**JIM**, *still massaging, opens his mouth as though to object before placing her hand deep into his mouth. He sucks on her fingers and flat of her hand as she continues.*)
>
> (*She likes the way this feels but is fighting it.*)

...
...
I loved the way people would look at us
at the movies
out shopping
sitting on our terrace for brunch.
There was always an intake of breath
and a triple take.
A look to you
then to me
then to you again
as though making sure they had to do the calculations
on what you look like in contrast to me
twice just to check their work.
Yet they always seemed so pleased
with their result.
You became this sort of champion
and I became Helen of Troy.
Beyoncé.
"So beautiful."
They have so many ways
to tell you
that you weren't at all
what they were expecting.
And our sex was good

KANEISHA. it was so good.
I remember being nervous
so afraid to see your dick
all pink
and shriveled.
A naked mole rat
swimming in hair
is what I imagined.
Or like a cucumaria...
that weird ocean thing
that like sea caterpillar
imagined that but pink.
But your dick was perfect.
So rigid and right
and we fit.
Nicely.
And the sex was good.
Very good.
Till three years ago.
That's when everything got bad.
...
...
Then it –
well it...
when I told my friends
they said
"that happens. That's every couple
just give it a few weeks.
A few months. DON'T CHEAT.
Just take some time...
Or see if he's into being open?
Are either of you tied to monogamy?
Maybe invite someone in?

Are you into women?
Have you tried choking?
A little rape play?
How are you spicing things up?
Fantasy is important."

> (**JIM** *begins to slowly take off* **KANEISHA**'s *shirt.*)

> (*"Work" by Rihanna begins to play loud again.*)

And I remember one day I woke up
and I screamed.
I woke you up.
Do you remember that?
I woke you up.
And I had screamed because I looked at you
and...
that fog again...
it sort of lifted
or shifted
the fog,
it sort of distorted
and I saw your face
and for the first time
you weren't foreign
you were just
you were white
a flesh and blood white
that I didn't know
and I was scared.
I was scared for my life.
But I was turned on.
Because it was like a stranger was in my bed.
and I remember you were all freaked out

KANEISHA. and you rolled over to hug me and I tensed
because I felt your erection against my side
and I...
it felt like a violation.
And then the fog shifted
and you were you again.
You.
With your accent
and your hands
touching me
with familiarity.
And I was me.
And so I put it away
that moment before
and it became something
fraught and erotic...
like this little secret
tucked away in the back of my mind
that gradually crystallized into
a hidden jewel I've coveted in my psychic space
for two years.
Two years...
because I didn't know what it meant.
Now I do.
That was...
The reason I was so attracted to this
Antebellum Sexual Performance Therapy
was because it gave me that electricity
on the back of my neck again
The minute I read about it.
and the electricity
always calmed my OCD
always.

And earlier today
it was calmed and I was feeling
naturally
as we were engaging in that fantasy play.
Because, baby,
I realized,
the elders watching me.
They are watching me lay in bed
every night with a demon
who thinks he's a saint.
And the elders don't care that you
are a demon,
they lay with them too…
they just want you to know it.
And me to know it.
So I can lie with grace.
So I can lie with their blessing
and if I don't have their blessing
this

–

…

I don't see a way for this to continue how it's been going.
Cause / you don't seem to –

> (**JIM** pushes **KANEISHA** face-first into the bed.)

JIM. Shut up you dirty negress.

KANEISHA. Jim?
What the / hell are you –

> (**JIM** rips the shirt **KANEISHA** had been wearing and stuffs her mouth closed.)
>
> ("Work" by Rihanna abruptly stops.)

JIM. I said
shut up,
you dirty
negress.

> (**JIM** *begins to pull the rest of* **KANEISHA**'s *clothes off. While also undoing his shirt and pants.*)

You're a nasty little bed wench who's been asking for this all day
ain'tcha?

> (**KANEISHA** *makes a muffled sound.*)
>
> (*Suddenly,* **JIM** *has a whip and slams it on the bedpost.*)

What the hell did I say wench?

> (**JIM** *takes off all his clothes and climbs on top of* **KANEISHA**. *He begins to lick her from her buttocks to the back of her head.*)
>
> (*Then he spits on her.*)

Taste like dirt.
That's bout all y'all can taste of.
which is a shame
cause chocolates are my favorite dessert.
But you don't know nothing bout that now do you?
Now listen up negress.
You been running your mouth for a good little time now
but when I look round this
damn room
I don't see nothing done
from a day's work
but a suitcase that's half packed
and a bed that's unmade.

Which leaves me thinking that you thought you could run away somewhere.
Is that what you thought?

> (**KANEISHA** *begins.*)

How many times do I have to tell you negress you don't get to talk
till I tell you to talk.

> (**JIM** *lifts the whip high in the air,* **KANEISHA** *screams.*)
>
> (**JIM** *begins to laugh hysterically.*)

You real black hefers are so dumb.
You think I'd put welts on ya
BEFORE I get up in ya?
You done lost your mind I reckon...
No I'm gonna take my time with you
give you what you need
get what I need
and then...
you'll get the beatin you've been waiting on.
Ya hear?
You can nod your head.

> (**KANEISHA** *and* **JIM** *stare at each other in a weighted silence. Slowly, she nods her head in the affirmative.*)

OK...
now...
bite down real hard
because I'm about to hurtcha
negress!

> (*Suddenly,* **JIM** *forcefully flips* **KANEISHA** *over, spreads her legs, and plunges forward.*

He's clutching her throat and pushing her face against the pillow.)

*(**KANEISHA** begins to fumble and fight as **JIM** thrusts into and out of her repeatedly. **KANEISHA**'s arms flail this way and that looking for something, anything to help her when she remembers that her nails are sharp and his chest is exposed. She begins to claw angrily at his chest, blood spewing everywhere till finally he's off!)*

*(**KANEISHA** lets out a scream that sends the gag falling out of her mouth and her body shivering from groin to skull.)*

KANEISHA. Starbucks!
Starbucks!
Starbucks!

*(**KANEISHA** falls off the bed and begins to cry. It is a full-bodied, all hands on deck type of cry.)*

*(**JIM** looks over to **KANEISHA**, not sure what came over him, not sure why he did what he did as the last light of the Virginia dusk begins to fade away and a slight breeze knocks their window against the pane.)*

*(**JIM** begins to crawl over to **KANEISHA** slowly when suddenly the all hands on deck cry becomes a guttural laugh. **KANEISHA** is overcome.)*

*(She rolls out of her spot next to the bed and crawls over to **JIM**, where she reaches over and kisses him. Tears begin to stream again, but this time from **JIM**'s ducts.)*

(It is an ocean of tears with waves, convulsions, and from its depths escapes a wail – warbling out from tumultuous guts.)

*(**KANEISHA** slowly moves away from him, pulling herself to her feet. And then...)*

(And then...)

(And then...)

*(The actress playing **KANEISHA** does whatever she feels is right before she looks to him.)*

Thank you, baby.
Thank you for listening.

End of Play

www.ingramcontent.com/pod-product-compliance
Lightning Source LLC
Chambersburg PA
CBHW072009290426
44109CB00018B/2187